A MOMENT IN TIME

Fifty stories that bring East Anglia's history to life

PETER SARGENT

A Moment in Time
Fifty stories that bring East Anglian history to life

First published in Great Britain in paperback, October 2017
by Paul Dickson, 8 Bridge Court, Fishergate, Norwich NR3 1UE
Tel: 01603 666011.
paul-dickson@btconnect.com

© 2017 Peter Sargent

The right of Peter Sargent to be identified as the author of this work has been asserted by him in accordance with the Copyright, Designs & Patents Act 1988.

All rights reserved. No part of this publication may be reproduced, stored in a retrieval system or transmitted in any form or by any means, electronic, mechanical, recording or otherwise, without the prior written permission of the author.

ISBN Paperback 978-0-9956187-1-8
ISBN E-book 978-0-9956187-2-5

A CIP catalogue record of this book is available from the British Library.

Cover design and illustrations by Annette Hudson.
Photographs by the author and courtesy of Peterborough Museum and Visit Essex.
Printed in Norwich by Swallowtail Print

To the memory of my late father, who loved a good history book.

Foreword

By **Neil Haverson**

Former editor, Let's Talk magazine and
Eastern Daily Press newspaper columnist

My history master at school had the ability to capture my interest in a subject that might otherwise have passed me by. I suspect this may have had something to do with the fact that he, like me, was a keen cricketer. He could be easily side-tracked, and the rise of Napoleon would morph into ten minutes on the England team selected for the Ashes Test.

Mixing the two subjects somehow helped me absorb more than I realised about the history of our nation and the rest of the world. Not to mention a greater understanding of the lbw law.

I worked with Peter Sargent in Norwich on Archant's Let's Talk magazine where I was editor and Peter the production editor. We worked hard but it was fun; we shared a similar sense of humour – and looking back I realise that period had parallels with my schooldays.

Peter's depth of knowledge of history and his ability to communicate it was a feature of our working day. Often he would come out with historical quotes. Or if I made a random comment he would inform me how this remark had its roots in history or who first said it.

Anything submitted for the magazine with an historical bent went straight to Peter's in-tray. Having read the copy, more often than not, he would say: "Ah yes and did you know…"

To commemorate the centenary of the start of the First World War we set out to produce three supplements in Let's Talk in 2014. They were to feature readers' memories of their relative's involvement, together with stories of the conflict and a timeline of significant events.

The project was handed to Peter. He planned, designed, edited and produced all three supplements. He researched the timelines, wrote articles and saw the whole thing off to the printers.

The result was three superb publications that garnered praise from both inside and outside the company.

From this book you will appreciate this knowledge Peter has and his ability to set it down in a way that makes it accessible to all.

His popular column in the Eastern Daily Press was perfect to sit with a coffee and read on a Saturday morning and be introduced to characters and facts from the region's past that many of us probably never knew existed.

History is, of course, a huge subject but Peter has selected a cross-section of fascinating stories that give us an insight into almost 2,000 years of our past. They will hook the interest and motivate the reader to want to find out more about how our region and its people have evolved over the centuries.

And to complete the parallel with my schooldays, Peter also has a keen interest in cricket. So my days with him as a friend and colleague on Let's Talk not only rebooted my interest in history, but prompted many a discussion on England's team for the Ashes Test.

Introduction

Most of the stories you will read in this book first saw life on the back page of the Eastern Daily Press newspaper's Weekend section.

While working as a night sub-editor I began writing short introductions to the lives of famous people from East Anglia – Nelson, Boudicca, Cromwell and so on – and found these characters only scratched the surface of an endlessly fascinating subject. Before long I found myself casting the net wider, taking in the more obscure people and places who made a mark on our region.

Tip-offs from readers and many of my work colleagues sent me off in search of out of the way monuments and roadside markers, of inscriptions in country churches as well as incidental illustrations of events in the middle of larger cities and towns. It's been a learning experience, and extremely rewarding.

For this collection I've selected 50 of my favourite stories. The style is conversational and, I hope, as entertaining as it is informative – imagine a couple of history enthusiasts discussing the subject, more than likely over a pint of foaming ale.

The content and chronology is – to say the least – varied; from ancient pagan artwork to Second World War troops training for D-Day. You might think this reflects a scatterbrain mind, or jackdaw tendencies, but, believe me, there is a logic to it all.

These fifty stories represent just a fraction of the fascinating little episodes that make up our history. If the locations and subject matter lean a little towards the city of Norwich and county of Norfolk, it is merely because I have been based in the city for the past 20 years – and also studied history at the University of East Anglia way back in the mid-1980s.

These stories and the characters in them range from the nationally important – Oliver Cromwell recruiting his Ironside cavalry troopers, Mary Tudor claiming the crown in a moment of high drama from a castle in Suffolk or Queen Elizabeth I conducting a grand tour of East Anglia – to those of merely local interest – 19th century eccentrics in Norfolk, raffish and courageous boxers of the Regency period or a post rammed into shrinking peatland in the middle of the fens. But they all show how national and international events we read about in the history book impact on ordinary people, and how they reacted.

For example, who were the craftsmen who created the beautifully painted saints on the Binham rood screen in the early 16th century only for others – perhaps their own descendants – to whitewash them within a generation? It all happened because of King Henry VIII's decisions taken at a national level, but it impacted upon the daily lives of humble people living in a village near the Norfolk coast.

That, for me, is what history is really about. The people higher up make the decisions, and the rest of us have to live with the consequences. That was the way then, and it still is today.

There are many people to thank. From my parents, who first introduced me to a love of history, through to some very good schoolteachers and my editors at the EDP, who gave me the chance to go off at a tangent. Thanks also to my publisher Paul Dickson, who has guided a first-time writer through the assault course of publishing a book, to Annette Hudson for the superb historical illustrations and book cover design – and to my friends at the Adam and Eve pub in Norwich for their encouragement, fresh ideas and patience in listening to me rattling on all these years! Any mistakes in the book are, of course, my own.

I hope these tales will entertain, as well as inform. I take the view that, if it interests me, it will interest others.

Peter Sargent
Norwich
August, 2017

Contents

Guide to pictures in colour section

Mysterious: A Green Man in the cloisters of Norwich Cathedral.

The Green Man

In the cloisters of Norwich Cathedral are some amazing carvings set in the roof space. Most feature familiar religious scenes, but peeping out from behind some foliage is the face of a man. These representations are found across England – and many other places around the world.

An odd character. . .

The origins of the Green Man are shrouded in mystery. There are many theories as to how he got here. A Green Man is a carved or sculpted figure, usually comprising a face emerging through foliage, or with roots coming out of his mouth. He is often found in churches, but can also be discovered in unexpected corners in other buildings. One in Norwich Cathedral has a strange expression that doesn't quite fit in among all the saints and holy figures around him. He has a wide-eyed look which some may find malevolent; others may see him as a little wild, a rustic, earthy sort of fellow at odds with his urban, civilised surroundings. Another in the cathedral looks more like a monk, with the haircut to match. The Green Man has come a long way in our imaginations, from prehistoric times, and the Middle Ages to a fresh interpretation in the 21st century.

Prehistoric?

At the most basic level, the Green Man can be seen as a god of fertility. His appearance – half man, half vegetable – could symbolise the turning of the seasons, the hope that crops will grow and feed the people, saving primitive societies from starvation. Images of the Green Man can be seen in all sorts of places in East Anglia; at churches such as St Nicholas, Blakeney, Castle Acre Priory, St Michael and All Angels, Aylsham and at Ely Cathedral; you'll also find him at the medieval gateway to Norwich Cathedral, the Ethelbert Gate, and at the 17th century Custom House at King's Lynn, as well as pubs, such as the Adam and Eve in Norwich. He can be glimpsed on some gravestones, carvings of skulls from which foliage is sprouting. A little macabre, perhaps, but as an image of rebirth the Green Man is a universal symbol. The crops in the ground emerge after the seeming death of winter, guaranteeing that life goes on. Spring sees the earth bloom again, in what must have seemed a miraculous, supernatural fashion to our ancestors. The Green Man has also been found throughout Europe and even in India, and has spread to North America. He was known to the ancient Greeks and Romans, to whom he was Bacchus, the god of wine and crops. For the ancient Celts he was the god of the abundant, life-giving spring. He crops up in English folklore in different guises. As well as carving and sculpture, the Green Man can be seen in stained glass or peeping out of the margins of old manuscripts.

What is a pagan character doing in churches?

The first Christian missionaries appealed to pagans by assimilating their old gods into the new religion. So many churches were built on the sites of former temples, and many country practices continued with new names. The Church may have considered it 'safer' to bring the old crop god in from the fields, and enlist his aid as a reassuring symbol. On a different level, the idea of the rebirth of crops may have struck a chord with the resurrection of Christ following His death at the crucifixion. Images have been found from the 11th to the 20th centuries. At other churches, they can be seen on the ends of pews and fonts, as well as in roofs. Typically, the Reformation frowned upon this kind of imagery, and Green Men ceased to appear in churches. The Victorians revived the fashion, though more as a decorative design to go with their Gothic Revival in churches. The Green Man was adopted with enthusiasm by the Arts and Crafts movement. Inspired by the writers John Ruskin and William Morris, this was a harking back to a pre-industrial past when people were much closer to nature. Green Men (and it is usually men, not women) featured in May Day celebrations. These ancient festivals celebrate the start of the spring, so it's not surprising to see a Green Man along with a May Queen at village processions. In the 19th century chimney sweeps invented the character of Jack-in-the-Green, a man inside a wicker framework covered with leaves who joined in their holiday celebrations. Jack and his followers got up to all sorts of tricks, trying to get money out of people. Eventually their rowdy behaviour was stamped out.

Any other links?

During the 14th century an anonymous poet wrote Sir Gawain and the Green Knight. Set during the Arthurian period, it tells the tale of a giant knight who appears at Camelot during a New Year feast. He is dressed all in green, with green skin, green beard, green armour, even a green horse. Clearly a supernatural figure, he issues a challenge which young Sir Gawain accepts. The epic goes on to chart Gawain's quest. The Green Man is a complex character; half monster, half hero, and is seen by historians as symbolic of Christianity's struggle with a pagan past. Some have even seen an echo of the Green Man in early depictions of Father Christmas. Before the modern fashion for illustrating him as an old man in a red suit, he was seen wearing green. He was associated with the abundance of gifts at Christmas, much as the pagan Green Man brought abundance of food. Another linked hero is Robin Hood. Robin and his outlaws, dressed in green, hid in the woods living off what nature (and the rich!) can give them. And don't forget Herne the Hunter. This fantastical creature was a woodland spirit, always pictured wearing stag antlers, half-human, half-animal. Fans of the 1980s TV serial Robin Hood will remember his mystical appearances in the forest.

And in modern times?

The Green Man is a popular pub name. The name has cropped up at Little Snoring, Rackheath, Briston and Wroxham Road, Norwich. In the 21st century there may be a new lease of life for the Green Man. He can be seen a characteristic of nature itself, fragile and endangered by the actions of humanity as we misuse the earth's resources.

1st century **47AD**

The Battle of Stonea

"The neighbouring tribes now chose a battlefield at a place protected by a rustic earthwork, with an approach too narrow for cavalry. The Romans broke through the embankment. The enemy, imprisoned by their barrier, were overwhelmed."
So wrote the Roman 1st century AD historian Tacitus. But where was this battle? Modern archaeologists believe it is probably the hill fort at Stonea, in the Cambridgeshire fens, close to the Norfolk border.

A hill fort. In the fens. Really?

Ridiculous as it sounds, Stonea Camp is the lowest hill fort in Britain. It might be more accurate to describe it as an "island fort". At two metres above sea level this is the closest to a hill you get in the fens. Archaeological investigations indicate the site has been occupied since Neolithic times (c5000-2500BC). The fort itself was most likely built between 350 and 100BC, and remained in use until the 1st century AD. It was on an island surrounded by wet fen, flooded land with reeds, sedges and a network of meres and streams. But this was far from uninhabitable land. At this time the area was far dryer than it became in the Middle Ages. Stonea, like the islands that later became such towns as Ely and March, stood out and became important to the Iron Age tribes.

Primitive lot, weren't they?

So Roman writers would have us believe. Modern research questions this. A Time Team documentary for Channel 4 a few years ago suggested that Britain in 43AD was a far more sophisticated society than hitherto thought, and recent archaeology backs this up. Divided into a series of tribal kingdoms, they had their own complicated politics, economy and perhaps even a class system. At Stonea, an excavation carried out by the British Museum in the 1980s discovered the defensive ditches on one side were 5m (15ft) wide and 1.8m deep with steep sides. Earth taken from these ditches was piled up to form large internal banks, topped up by wooden palisades. On the other side, the ditches were flooded with fen water, creating defences. Within this large site only a privileged elite lived. They may have been the king and his family protected by aristocratic household warriors, or perhaps they were a religious caste. Supplies and labour came from surrounding farms – peasants and gentry? The fort became a place of sanctuary for the surrounding population in times of danger, when invaders threatened. We don't know enough about Iron Age society to judge, but some of their customs

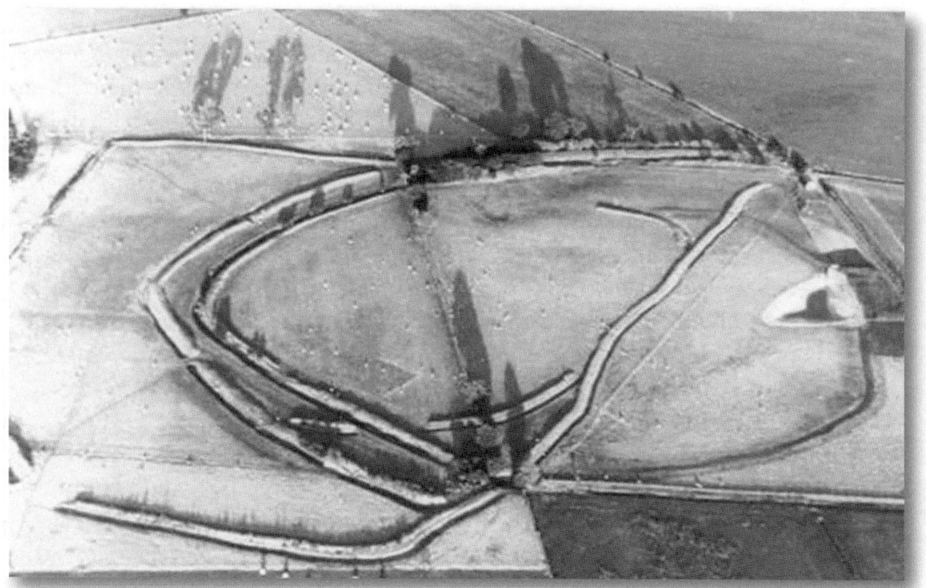

Stronghold: Aerial view of Stonea Camp, showing the fortifications in a 'D' shape.
Picture: Dr Ben Robinson

may have been abhorrent to us. Archaeologists discovered the skull of a four-year-old child buried in the ditch. Sword marks were cut deeply into it. "I found the child's remains in the base of a ditch during the first season – a very sobering experience," said Dr Ben Robinson, of Peterborough Museum and Art Gallery. "I think these could be battle massacre wounds (especially the glancing blow at the top of the skull), but they are not necessarily associated with the Roman troubles. The remains seem to pre-date that (the radiocarbon dates just don't fit). Late Iron Age Britain was a violent place at times, and it would not surprise me if the 'borderland' site at Stonea saw inter-tribe warfare and raiding. Equally, I am sure that the site functioned as some kind of spiritual or administrative centre – it does not feel domestic."

What about this battle?

The Romans invaded Britain in 43AD. They met stiff resistance in the south and west, but in the east the Iceni, ruled by their king Prasutagus, made a pragmatic peace with the invaders. Nevertheless, four years later, there was an uprising among the Iceni. It may have been led by a dissident branch of the tribe – we might today say patriots against collaborators. The Iceni heartland, however, was in west Norfolk. "It is in the extreme west of Iceni territory in a landscape that might have been occupied by any of the three major tribes," said Dr Robinson, adding coin finds indicated it was an Iceni site, though these could, of course, have been stolen. Roman governor Ostorius Scapula led his legions against the insurgents, and quickly defeated them. A site at Saham Toney has been suggested as their royal headquarters. This reinforces the view that the tribe was divided. Stonea's defences were no match for the well-drilled legionaries. They had already taken the more imposing hill fort at South Cadbury in Somerset, so the fortifications in the fens would have caused them few real problems. After the battle Prasutagus ruled peacefully enough, the Romans settled a colony to the south at Colchester and the Iceni king even made the emperor his heir. Fourteen years later, it all went horribly wrong when he died and his widow and family were mistreated by the Romans. She was Boudicca, and her revenge was breathtaking.

What happened at Stonea?

Following Boudicca's defeat, the Romans created a town there. It is the only Roman town found in the fens. Although not as important as that south of Norwich – Venta Icenorum – it became an administrative centre. Archaeologists discovered the remains of a two-storey tall, six-metre square tower heated by an underground system known as a hypocaust next to the old fort. Stonea Grange was an imperial estate for Emperor Hadrian, who visited Britain in 122AD. It existed until the third century.

What about the fort?

The embankments remained largely untouched for 2,000 years. During the Middle Ages the land belonged to the Abbot of Ely, and was known as Stitches Farm. More intense agriculture during the 1970s disrupted things. Deep ploughing and use of chemicals destroyed the old defences. However, following the British Museum's 1980s dig, it was bought by Cambridgeshire County Council in 1990, and the embankments rebuilt. Now a scheduled monument, it's a peaceful place, populated only by sheep.

■ Stonea Camp is open to the public, signposted down a single track off the bumpy B1098 road between Manea and Wimblington.

Forts of the Saxon shore

"The work of giants is crumbling." So it may have seemed to fifth century Saxon peasants as they looked on the crumbling walls of the mighty Roman forts built along the east coast.

Was it really that simple?

We used to think so. The old school textbooks were precise. 410AD, Romans leave, 450AD Saxons move in. Today the story does not look so clear. A similar story could be told for the forts the later Roman Empire built along its vulnerable east coast. From The Wash

Roman ruin: The high walls of Burgh Castle.

down to what is now Portsmouth in the south a string of fortifications went up that were inhabited for up to 200 years. Remains at such sites as Brancaster, Caister and Burgh Castle provoke many questions. Why were they built? Against whom? When were they abandoned? Archaeologists are searching for clues, historians are divided on the answers.

What was the Saxon Shore?
The name comes from the Count of the Saxon Shore. He was the Roman commander with the responsibility of keeping the coast of Britannia safe in the third and fourth centuries. Rome had conquered southern Britain after 43AD. A period of prosperity – the *pax Romanica* – followed. But after 200 years of imperial rule the picture looked different. Internal chaos and civil war within, and barbarians knocking on the doors without, led to a more defensive regime. By the 280s Britain had a separatist ruler named Carausius. He defied Rome and it took a decade to put down the revolt. In the following century others followed, as Rome's authority weakened. Forts were built. Brancaster was probably the first, in the early 200s. Caister and Burgh Castle followed later in the century. They were built on the coast of what was then a vast tidal estuary, now modern Yarmouth. They faced each other across the water, part of a series of military sites and lighthouses.

Were they like medieval castles?
These were solid constructions. At Burgh Castle the walls were of flint with tiles to hold it together. Three sides remain, with several projecting bastions, the fourth wall having collapsed into the marsh. The walls are 9ft thick and at least 14ft high. These forts, the last word in contemporary military engineering, were built to withstand a siege. There is little to see now at Brancaster and Caister, where a thorough demolition job over the centuries has left little but the foundations. More rewarding for the observer are the great fortifications at Burgh Castle. Archaeologists point out that coastal erosion and siltation have changed the landscape so much they distort the reason the forts were built where they were. The estuary of the Yare, for example, was wider 2,000 years ago; Caister would have been on a small island. At Brancaster the fort was closer to the beach than it is today, while Burgh now looks over Breydon Water, the remains of the once huge estuary. At Walton on the Suffolk coast the Roman castle long ago crumbled into the sea. There is evidence of another fort at Skegness, also washed away by the erosion that is still a factor on this coast.

What function did the forts serve?
The likeliest explanation is that they were to thwart barbarian Saxon seaborne raids from what is now northern Germany. At the same time the walls at Venta

Icenorum, the Roman market town near modern Norwich, went up. Some bold historians beg to differ; they suggest they were built by British separatists against imperial retribution and that the threat from barbarians has been exaggerated with the benefit of hindsight. Others say they were fortified ports, engaged in trade with the greater empire but with an eye to security. We don't really know. It is more likely they were built by the army or navy and garrisoned by troops against the Saxon threat.

What was life like in the forts?

In all three of the Norfolk forts remains of internal buildings have been destroyed. There would have been a principia (headquarters) a bath-house, of course, as well as living quarters. Wives and children may have lived within the walls. By the time of the later empire much of the army was made up of 'barbarians' living within the empire, many of them from Germanic tribes. At Burgh there was a contingent of elite Greek cavalry who may have formed a mobile "rapid reaction force" to act quickly against pirates in the marshes, while at Brancaster there was a Dalmatian (modern Croatian) unit. Aerial photography has shown up dwellings outside the forts – service industries feeding the garrisons – as well as evidence of agriculture. Suggestions that a 500-strong complement within a space of roughly seven acres may have been housed at each fort are not implausible, though that may have been a peak number in times of emergency.

When were the forts abandoned?

By the early fifth century Roman authority was crumbling. Whether due to internal or external pressures people began abandoning Roman towns and fortresses in Britain. Some sites were deserted. At Burgh the walls were adapted and later became part of a Norman castle. The seventh century Saxon saint Fursey was associated with the site. But for humble peasants who lived in small wooden buildings, these Roman walls must have looked like the work of vanished giants.

■ Further reading: The Roman Shore Forts (Andrew Pearson, Tempus, 2002). Burgh Castle's walls are cared for by English Heritage, the rest of the fort owned by the Norfolk Archaeology Trust. The castle is west of Yarmouth, and attracts many nature lovers.
www.englishheritage.org.uk; www.norfarchtrust.org.uk

9th century **869**

The tale of Saint Edmund

King and martyr, first patron saint of England and last ruler of the independent kingdom of East Anglia. That much we know about King Edmund – the rest is legend.

Killed by the Vikings, wasn't he?

In November, 869 the Danish Vikings conquered East Anglia. According to most versions of the legend, King Edmund, aged about 28, was captured. The Danes offered to save his life if he gave up his kingdom and renounced Christianity. He refused to do either. The Danes tortured him, tied him to a tree, shot him to death with arrows and, finally, beheaded him and dumped his body. Eventually, English villagers found the body, but not the head. They heard a plaintive call of "Here! Here!" from the forest, followed the sounds, and there was the head calling. It was sheltered between the paws of a huge wolf. The wolf allowed the people to pick up the head, then followed them to where the body was, and watched until head was united to body and properly buried. Satisfied, it headed back into the trees. The legend of Edmund the Martyr was born. People began to venerate the site of burial, which became a place of pilgrimage. Eventually it was moved in state to the town of Beodricesworth – later Bury St Edmunds. Edmund was England's patron saint for more than 400 years.

Any truth to the legend?

The facts are fragmentary, and later embellishments make it hard to decide not only where Edmund died, but where his remains ended. Two sources dominate; the near contemporary Anglo-Saxon Chronicle, admirably concise, but infuriatingly brief, and a tenth century biography written by a monk called Abbo of Fleury, who added colour to the story. Abbo said Edmund was of "old Saxon stock", which could have meant he came from Germany. Aged 14 he sailed to England to take up the East Anglian throne, and landed at Hunstanton. There a chapel was later built for him, and the king has been associated with the site ever since. Another legend suggests he spent a year in religious seclusion there – though others say he lived at either Attleborough, Reedham or even Aldborough on the Suffolk coast. He was crowned on Christmas Day, 855.

Trouble on the way. . .

The threat of Norse invasion loomed. In 865 the Danes first wintered in East

Howling good tale: A sculpture of the wolf that led to Edmund's body stands by the ruins of St Edmund's Chapel in Hunstanton.

Anglia. Four years later, having taken Northumbria and much of the midlands, they were back to stay, led by Ubbe Ragnarsson and Ivar the Boneless. The Chronicle says: *"Edmund the king fought against them and the Danes took the victory, killed the king and overcame all the land."* The decisive battle may have been at Thetford, which was the Danes' headquarters. Other legends say Edmund was besieged at either Old Buckenham or Framlingham, but escaped. On the run, he hid from the Danes beneath Goldbrook bridge in the village of Hoxne. Spotted by a newly-wed couple who saw his spurs reflected in moonlight, he was betrayed. Abbo said the king, like Christ, refused to fight – but embraced martyrdom. *"Thus the heathens led the faithful king to a tree firmly rooted in Earth, tightened him thereto with sturdy bonds, and scourged him for a long time with straps. He always called*

between the blows with belief in truth to Christ the Saviour."
Other places besides Hoxne claim to be the site of Edmund's martyrdom; Hellesdon near Norwich was known as Hailesun, a similar spelling to the place named by the Chronicle. A number of other spots in Suffolk have their claims. Perhaps the most telling evidence in Hoxne's favour is its proximity to Edmund's final resting place. For many years a tree stood in the village, said to be the one to which he was tied.

The legend becomes a fact

As tales of miracles grew, so did the saint's aura. About 40 years after his death, as the English began to reconquer the Danelaw, his remains were moved to a grand new abbey. At Bury St Edmunds, the Edmund industry took off. People travelled to venerate the saint; viewing parings of his nails, locks of hair, his shirt, banner and sword were highlights of the trip. Clerics swore his body was miraculously uncorrupted. In the early years of the 11th century the Vikings once again threatened; when they landed in force at Ipswich in 1010 Edmund's body was moved for safety to London. Even tough, pagan Vikings weren't immune to the legend. Three years later Sweyn Forkbeard had seized the English crown and arrived at Bury St Edmunds, to where the saint's body had been returned. As he prepared to attack the town and steal its treasure, he saw a vision of the saint in the air above him – and fell down dead. (Unfortunately, more prosaic records insist Sweyn died at Gainsborough, Lincolnshire. Spoilsports). The legend remained powerful. Sweyn's son Canute became king, and took the hint. A few years later he built a new stone church to house Edmund's relics.

Don't mess with the saint!

The stories grew with the telling; there was the sacrilegious monk who tried to test whether the saint's head was attached to his body – and was struck dumb for his cheek. There was the nobleman dying of plague restored to life by the sight of the body. The abbey at Bury grew rich on pilgrims. Edmund was honoured for centuries; Henry V's army carried his banner at Agincourt in 1415, but he had by then been replaced as England's patron saint when Edward III favoured Saint George in 1349. At the Reformation in 1538, Bury abbey was dismantled, but there was no sign of his body. One tale went that he had been taken to Toulouse in France 300 years previously, but some say he is still buried in the grounds of the abbey, with his treasure. In May, 2017, new clues indicated he may still be buried in a monks' graveyard underneath what are now tennis courts in the abbey grounds. A campaign to reinstate him as our patron saint has been launched in Suffolk, while a few years ago a sculpture of the wolf was unveiled by the ruins of St Edmund's Chapel, Hunstanton. Edmund took many secrets beyond the grave – but his legend lives on.

10th century **991**

Brithnoth's last stand

In this year Ipswich was harried and very soon afterwards ealdorman Brithnoth was slain at Maldon. In this year it was decided for the first time to pay tribute to the Danes because of the great terror they inspired along the sea coast. On this occasion it amounted to 10,000 pounds.

In these bare sentences the contemporary Anglo-Saxon Chronicle describes one of the most dramatic events of the Viking invasion of England. What happened at Maldon, on the East Anglian coast in 991AD, is a tale of great heroism and selflessness – or a military blunder, depending on your point of view. It had great significance for the future of the country.

Stalwart: Brithnoth is depicted in a statue on the promenade in Maldon.
Picture: Courtesy Visit Essex

Not those pesky Vikings again?

The Norse raiders had first appeared in Britain at the end of the eighth century. During the middle of the ninth century they came close to conquering the whole of England; only the intervention of Alfred the Great prevented that. A century later England appeared safe from the Vikings. Alfred's warrior successors had united the country under a single king, and the nation was wealthy and secure. Or not, as it turned out. The succession of a boy king, 10-year-old Ethelred, in 979, destabilised the country. Two years later, according to the Chronicle, "for the first time seven ships came and ravaged Southampton". Thanet, Cheshire and Padstow got the same treatment. The Vikings were back.

And no doubt they meant business

The defences of the country had been run down, and under a boy king there was no central leadership. Everything was down to the men on the spot. The ealdormen – the Norse equivalent was an earl – were the chief noblemen of the shires. They were assisted by thanes, lesser nobles, and backed up by their housecarls, household warriors, professionals who were devoted to their lord. In Anglo-Saxon armies they were the bedrock of the force, wielding their mighty war axes to great effect. Landowners, friends and family of the ealdorman, would bring their own followers. The mass of the army was composed of the fyrd, a militia of ordinary men raised from the peasantry. Occasionally fierce, but poorly equipped and armed, they needed strong leadership. Such was the force that, in August, 991, was mobilised to meet a new threat. A fleet of 93 ships, under Olaf Tryggvason the Norwegian king, ravaged the East Anglian shore as far as Ipswich. Ealdorman Brithnoth gathered the fyrd to oppose them at the estuary of the River Blackwater. The subsequent drama was immortalised by a later epic poem. While it may add some 'spin' to events, the essential truth comes through. The anonymous author says that the Vikings had landed on an island off the Essex coast, possibly Northey Island. This sat in a sea of tidal mudflats, joined to the mainland by a causeway flooded at high tide. Separated by the water, the two sides engaged in some traditional pre-battle banter – threats, bad language and mockery. At 65 years old, Brithnoth was an old man, certainly by the standards of the day. Very much a traditionalist, this tall, imposing figure responded to the Vikings' taunts about paying them tribute in the form of gold. "We will give you spears for tribute . . . you shall not win treasure so easily", thundered the old warrior. The Vikings could not cross the causeway, and even a small number of English warriors could have stopped them had they tried. Then, astonishingly, the Vikings asked Brithnoth if they could cross – and he said yes.

Very sporting. . .

Typically English, you might say. Why did he do it? Was he over-confident of success, or was he spoiling for a fight to avenge the destruction at Ipswich? Or is it possible the poet made this bit of the story up, to make it a better tale? The English were outnumbered. One version of the story, based on the number of ships in the fleet, maintains the Vikings had 2,000 men, Brithnoth just 200. This could be more poetic licence to make the odds greater. The Vikings, on shore in force, made for the tall figure of Brithnoth, hacking through his friends and relatives, and he was killed. Much of the fyrd fled at this point, but the ealdorman's housecarls fought to the death around the body of their lord. The poet quotes one of the warriors, the veteran Byrthwold, steadying his comrades: "Here lies our leader all hewn down, the valiant man in the dust; may he lament forever who thinks now to turn from this battle. I am old in age; I will not hence, but I purpose to lie by the side of my lord, by the man so dearly loved." True to their duty, the English died hard in the marshes.

Good story. Did it really happen?

Some observers say the poem is just a tale, an account written years later based on hearsay and legend. But it has an accurate ring, and the use of a number of specific names implies the characters were well-known to the poem's audience. In 1066 King Harold's own housecarls fought to the last man at Hastings even after their king had been killed. Making a last stand around the dead body of a fallen leader was not just a poetic convention.

What happened after the battle?

Brithnoth's body was recovered, and buried at Ely Cathedral. Maldon was just a preliminary skirmish in a long series of similar battles. In despair, Ethelred bribed the Danes with gold to leave – the Danegeld – but this show of weakness only encouraged them to return time after time. Coastal counties were harried for a generation. In 1004 it was the turn of Norwich and Thetford, pillaged and burnt by Viking armies. Ulfkell 'the Valiant', the new East Anglian ealdorman, also confronted them – and died in a battle near Thetford in which "the flower of the East Anglian people was killed". Eventually, following the death of Ethelred and his son, the Danish Canute took the crown of England.

■ **Further reading: In Search of the Dark Ages, Michael Wood**

Hereward the Wake and the Vikings

Thus was the minster of Peterborough burnt down and plundered. . . Hereward with his men joined them and they did all manner of evil deeds. When bishop Aethelric heard tell of this he excommunicated all the men who had done the evil deed.

In these words the Anglo-Saxon Chronicle recorded the Danish sacking of Peterborough in 1070.

Those rotten, rotten Vikings!
The Church rather expected this sort of behaviour when Scandinavian warbands came sailing into England. But the monks were more upset by the fact they were allied to an Englishman – Hereward the Wake. This great East Anglian folk hero, who led guerilla resistance against the conquering Normans from his base in the fens, was not universally popular. He received a generally bad press from many in the priesthood who, of course, wrote the only annals that survive. Hereward's is a mysterious story, part historical fact, but largely legend, tied to the tragic tale of England's resistance to William the Conqueror. Every 'fact' written about Hereward has to be taken with a substantial pinch of salt.

Hero or villain?
Most of us have him filed fair and square under 'hero'. His roots were in south Lincolnshire, the manor of Bourne to be precise. Some accounts, beginning with the 19th century author Charles Kingsley, reckoned him the son of an earl. A wild youth, he was banished or went voluntarily into exile. After various adventures (talking bears figure prominently) in the north country he ended up in Flanders. There he prospered, and married an heiress, said to be an enchantress. He was out of England during the Norman invasion of 1066, only returning home afterwards, by which time William the Conqueror had been crowned king. But discontent was only just beginning, fuelled by Norman atrocities. The legend goes that Hereward found his brother slaughtered and Normans feasting in his old home at Bourne. Accompanied by one Saxon axeman, he entered the hall and killed every

Plunder: Hereward saves a lady from the sack of Peterborough, according to this dramatic 19th century illustration.

Frenchman there. This was the beginning of the East Anglian revolt. At this point Hereward enters recorded history for the first time. The revolt against William drew support from the surviving English earls Edwin and Morcar, and also from Scandinavia.

Enter the Vikings

In 1066 Norway's Harold Hardrada had tried to seize England for himself, only to be killed at Stamford Bridge in Yorkshire. Now a Danish fleet was sniffing around the coast, sensing opportunity. The wide rivers of eastern England had been a highway for invasion before, and they were again. The Chroniclers wrote:

"King Swein came from Denmark into the Humber; the folk of the land came to meet him and made peace with him, believing he would overcome the land. Then the Danish bishop, Christian, came into Ely and the Danish housecarls [warriors] with him. The English folk of the fenlands came to them."

The fenmen's leader was Hereward, referred to by the Chronicle as "Hereward and his band". The allies headed for Peterborough, lying on the River Nene at the edge of the fens. They had the abbey in their sights.

Hereward was an enemy of the monks?

According to legend his uncle Brand was abbot of Peterborough, and had knighted Hereward at the beginning of the rebellion. But he died around 1069. King William took the opportunity to replace him with a French abbot named Turold – "a very hard man". Peterborough was known as the 'Golden Borough', such was the quantity and quality of the treasures kept there. Avaricious eyes turned their gaze on the poorly defended abbey. On June 1, 1070, Turold, at the head of about 200 mounted Frenchmen reached Stamford, west of Peterborough. He was met by one of the monks, Yware, who warned him the abbey was about to be attacked. The Chronicle tells the tale: "In the morning came all the outlaws with many ships and meant to enter the monastery; the monks withstood them so that they could not come in. Then they set fire to it, burnt all the monks' houses and all the town. By means of fire they came in at the Bolhithe Gate." Scorning the monks' attempts to surrender the raiders seized gold and silver sacred objects, along with "so many treasures in money, cloth and books that no man could reckon it to another; and they said they did it in loyalty to the monastery". Turold arrived too late, to find the monastery in ruins.

Was this what really happened?

This is the monks' own account, written up after the deed, and no doubt influenced by the new Norman regime. So they were unlikely to be favourable to Hereward. In his defence it can be said he may have been trying to protect the abbey from the Normans, fearing that Turold was coming to seize treasure for himself. It seems more likely that he was unable to control his Norse allies. Their subsequent conduct confirms this view. Making off with the loot they abandoned their English allies, making a truce with William. Hereward and the rebels holed up in the Isle of Ely, where they defied William for at least another year. The isle was a formidable fortress, surrounded by treacherous wetlands of the fens, and many Norman knights died trying to take it. Eventually, say the chronicles, it was the English abbot of Ely who betrayed the defenders by showing the Normans a safe crossing. Hereward and a few of his diehards escaped by boat. At this point they leave history behind – and enter legend. Although sources do not agree, it seems that following various Robin Hood-style adventures in the woods around Bourne, Hereward made his peace with the Conqueror. But jealous Norman knights had neither forgiven nor forgotten his rebellion. The best version – the one written by Charles Kingsley – describes an abandoned Hereward fighting against impossible odds, dying a hero's death. He was then buried secretly at night in Crowland Abbey. Presumably, he wouldn't have been welcome in Peterborough.

Anarchy in the fenland

"Never before had there been greater wretchedness in the country. . . and they said openly that Christ and His saints slept"
(The Peterborough Chronicle).

The 1140s has a good claim to be the worst decade in English history. Anarchy, bloodshed, famine and treachery thrived. Nowhere were things worse than in the fenland, where sites such as Cambridge and Ely felt the full force of the troubles.

Chronicle: The monks of Peterborough told the bloodthirsty tale of medieval anarchy in the fens during the period of civil war in the 1140s.

Well, the Middle Ages was a violent time.
Although medieval Englishmen were used to a degree of violence, they also treasured the law. With good reason. Without it they were subject to gangs of armed robbers who would plunder them without mercy. Sometimes these were the very men whose social position should have made them chivalrous protectors of the nation. Of all of these robber barons, none had a worse reputation than Geoffrey de Mandeville, First Earl of Essex, also known as "the devil in human form".

Sounds ominous. . .
In 1139 civil war broke out. King Henry I's daughter Matilda (or Maud) was meant to have inherited the crown on her father's death four years earlier, but she was successfully challenged by Henry's nephew, Stephen. He was a renowned warrior, and many knights felt able to renounce their vows to Matilda and back him instead. It was the cue for more than a decade of inconclusive fighting in which the English people were the losers. Many, though not all, of the aristocracy made a mockery of their supposed chivalry and honour by shamelessly changing sides. They plundered people who had no recourse to law when the rule of law had

Ransacked: Ramsey Abbey felt the full force of Geoffrey de Mandeville and his followers. Pictured is the gatehouse, all that remains these days of this once wealthy institution.

given way to naked violence. Geoffrey de Mandeville's father was a powerful nobleman who had quarrelled with Henry I, and subsequently lost his position as Constable of the Tower of London as well as valuable lands and castles. Mandeville's subsequent behaviour occurred in the light of his ambition to win his family's position back. This meant more to him than allegiance to any royal figure or the state of England. Nineteenth century historian J H Round reckoned he was "the most perfect and typical presentment of the feudal and anarchic spirit that stamps the reign of Stephen".

Who did he back – Stephen or Matilda?

Stephen. . . er Matilda, then Stephen again. Actually, he was backing himself while being bought by both with promises of land and position. Stephen's defeat and capture at Lincoln in February, 1141, led Mandeville to switch sides to Matilda. She gave him back his lands and position at the Tower. It was an important post, which he abused, and was hated by Londoners. As Stephen's fortunes improved, he defected again, being made Earl of Essex. But his faithlessness and brutality stretched the trusting and chivalrous Stephen's patience too far. Aware that Mandeville was even now negotiating with Matilda, the king again confiscated his castles. Mandeville became an outlaw.

Head for the hills!

The fens, actually. The near-impenetrable marshlands covering parts of Norfolk, Cambridgeshire and Lincolnshire were as much a refuge in 1143 as they had been in the times of Hereward the Wake 70 years earlier. Bandits and outlaws could hole up there for years, particularly when central and local government were in tatters. Abandoning his family's traditional lands in Middlesex, Essex and Hertfordshire, Mandeville headed for the one place he knew he would be safe from retribution. Accompanied by a rag-tag 'army' of mercenaries and rogues,

Mandeville wreaked havoc. First he seized Ely and garrisoned it. Next victim was the wealthy abbey at Ramsey. The monks were expelled, and the abbey plundered of its considerable treasure. From these two near-impregnable island bases Mandeville launched his men on raids across the region. Cambridge was sacked and burnt, people tortured to reveal where they had hidden treasure. The death toll rose. It was said that for a radius of 30 miles there was not a plough or oxen to be seen, as farmers abandoned their land in terror. Famine soon broke out. Monkish chronicler Henry of Huntingdon, warming perhaps a little too much to his story, later recorded that at Ramsey "blood exuded from the walls of the Church and the cloisters adjoining, witnessing to the divine indignation and prognosticating the destruction of the impious."

Did nobody try to stop it?

With the country in the grip of civil war, there were scant resources available. It had taken the whole army of William the Conqueror to winkle out Hereward's guerillas 70 years earlier, and a similar effort seemed necessary to defeat Mandeville. Fortunately, his reign of terror was relatively short-lived. In September, 1144, he was besieging Burwell Castle, near Cambridge. A stray arrow hit him, and he died. With him perished his reign of terror. As the church had excommunicated him for his many sins, he was denied burial. His body was wrapped in lead and taken to the headquarters of the Templar order in London. Later he was buried in their chapel there, and an effigy placed in the floor where it can be seen today.

What happened next?

Mandeville's son, also called Geoffrey, called off the troops and later paid the monks generous reparations. The monks went home to Ely and Ramsey, and life gradually returned to normal. In the country as a whole sporadic warfare only died out when Stephen agreed a compromise to support Matilda's young son. He became Henry II. His reign was characterised by attempts to strengthen English law, and thus avoid a return to 'The Anarchy', as the period became known. The final words can go to the anonymous monks who wrote the Peterborough Chronicle:

"In the days of this King there was nothing but strife, evil, and robbery, for quickly the great men who were traitors rose against him. When the traitors saw that Stephen was a good-humoured, kindly, and easy-going man who inflicted no punishment, then they committed all manner of horrible crimes . . . And so it lasted for nineteen years while Stephen was King, till the land was all undone and darkened with such deeds, and men said openly that Christ and his angels slept".

The barons, Bury and Magna Carta

England has not been successfully invaded since 1066 – or so we've been told. Yet Prince Louis of France had a pretty good go in the 1200s. Norwich was among the places he seized.

Oh no, not more sacking and looting!

King John (r1199-1216) was one of the least effective kings England ever had. Not only did he lose his lands in Normandy, his treasure in The Wash and get his country excommunicated by the pope, he also ended up with his rebel barons inviting a French prince to rule, and bring his army with him. From 1216-17 Louis controlled most of southern and eastern England. Norwich was among the castles he took from John, and its citizens bore the brunt of an occupying foreign army. Some modern historians make the case for Louis to be counted as one of the kings of England.

What? A Frenchman!

It's not so far-fetched. To the Angevin kings of England, with their roots in southern France, this northern island was little more than an adjunct to their main empires in continental Europe. They barely spoke the 'barbarous' English language. Ever since the Norman conquest of 1066, kings of England had spoken French as a first tongue and Latin as a second; the English were second class citizens. For many people, swapping one French-speaking overlord for another was a like-for-like deal. John – or Jean – succeeded his warrior brother, Richard I, in 1199. He had long been at odds with him, particularly during Richard's enforced absence while a prisoner in Germany on his way back from the crusades. As king of both England and Normandy, John proved a disaster. He lost his family's ancestral lands in Normandy to French king Philip – and was known as John 'Lackland' thereafter. Worse for his English subjects, his dispute with Pope Innocent III led to the whole country being placed under an 'interdict' by Rome. For seven years the church doors of England were shut as the whole country was effectively excommunicated. John's arbitrary rule alienated people throughout England. Things came to a head in 1214 when he faced a revolt by his own barons.

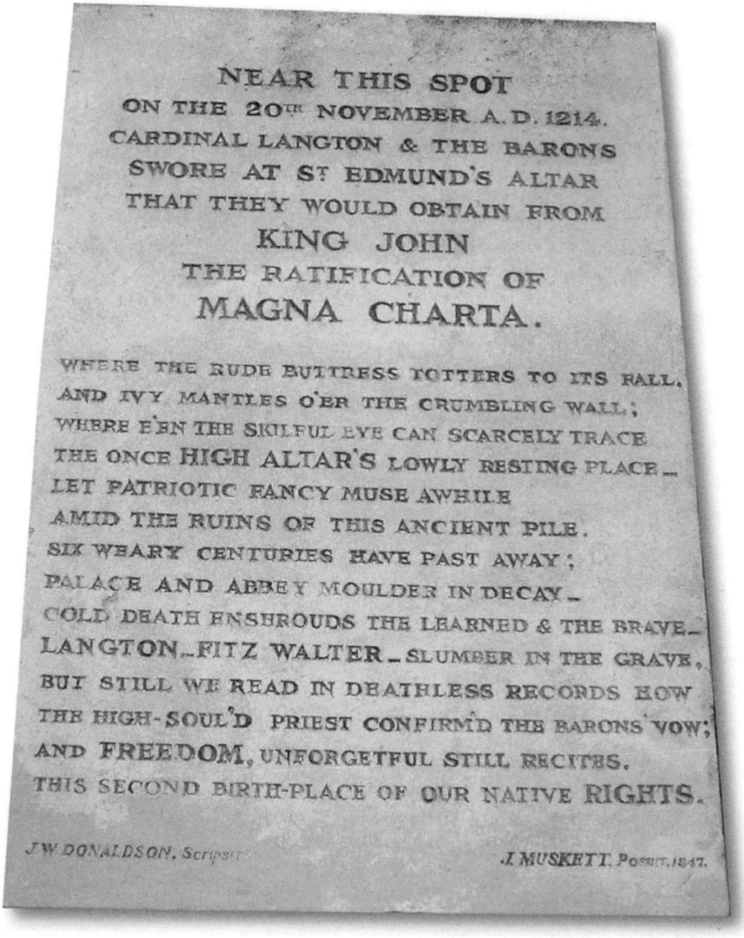

NEAR THIS SPOT
ON THE 20TH NOVEMBER A.D. 1214.
CARDINAL LANGTON & THE BARONS
SWORE AT ST EDMUND'S ALTAR
THAT THEY WOULD OBTAIN FROM
KING JOHN
THE RATIFICATION OF
MAGNA CHARTA.

WHERE THE RUDE BUTTRESS TOTTERS TO ITS FALL,
AND IVY MANTLES O'ER THE CRUMBLING WALL;
WHERE E'EN THE SKILFUL EYE CAN SCARCELY TRACE
THE ONCE HIGH ALTAR'S LOWLY RESTING PLACE –
LET PATRIOTIC FANCY MUSE AWHILE
AMID THE RUINS OF THIS ANCIENT PILE.
SIX WEARY CENTURIES HAVE PAST AWAY;
PALACE AND ABBEY MOULDER IN DECAY –
COLD DEATH ENSHROUDS THE LEARNED & THE BRAVE –
LANGTON – FITZ WALTER – SLUMBER IN THE GRAVE,
BUT STILL WE READ IN DEATHLESS RECORDS HOW
THE HIGH-SOUL'D PRIEST CONFIRM'D THE BARONS' VOW;
AND FREEDOM, UNFORGETFUL STILL RECITES,
THIS SECOND BIRTH-PLACE OF OUR NATIVE RIGHTS.

J.W. DONALDSON, Scripsit — J. MUSKETT. Posuit. 1847.

Set in stone: The inscription in the grounds of Bury St Edmunds Abbey.

A revolting lot!

The abbey at Bury St Edmunds played a vital part. John had kept the office of abbot vacant for a long time in order to keep its revenue for himself, and had thus angered the monks. In November, 1214, a group of nobles and clergy staged a dramatic meeting in the abbey church. They included the Archbishop of Canterbury, Stephen Langton, and Roger Bigod, Earl of Norfolk, whose locally powerful family had often been at odds with the monarchy. In all, 25 barons swore at the high altar they would force the king to sign a charter of liberties. They rallied support, took London and forced John to agree to the momentous document known as Magna Carta (Great Charter) the following year. Although now hailed as the cornerstone of our legal freedoms and constitution, the document was not intended so. It was more a move to bolster the rights of the aristocracy than an early move towards democracy. However, in its insistence that the crown could not arbitrarily imprison its subjects without recourse to the law it did establish a principle that has been upheld. When these days we debate such legal issues as imprisoning terrorist suspects, critics hark back to Magna Carta.

Didn't work out for John though.

The king had sealed the Charter under duress, and it was clear the peace would not hold. Across the Channel his enemies in France took due note. When he repudiated the truce, the rebels continued their struggle. This time they invited Prince Louis to come to their aid, with promises of the crown. He came, along with an army, in May, 1216. Many welcomed him as a saviour from the hated John. Gerald of Wales wrote: "The madness of slavery is over, the time of liberty has been granted, English necks are free from the yoke." Helped by willing English allies, Louis encountered little resistance as he marched through southern England, including Norfolk. He was unable to take the vital castle of Dover though. This was the situation when John died suddenly in 1216. He had already lost his crown jewels in The Wash, probably near modern day Sutton Bridge according to legend, and died at Newark, Lincolnshire, on October 19.

Why didn't Louis win?

The country seemed to have two kings. John's young son Henry was acclaimed in the west and midlands, while the east and south largely backed Louis. He initially prospered, but was defeated at sea, and support switched towards Henry III. Louis signed a peace treaty at Kingston, accepting a secret pay-off of 10,000 marks to leave these shores. In France, he succeeded his father, Philip, and became Louis VIII. Also known as the 'Lionheart', he pursued a successful military career.

What about this 'king of England' claim?

It's strange that this episode has been largely forgotten in our history, as it contradicts the claim that England has not been successfully invaded since 1066. Although uncrowned, Louis occupied much of England, and was recognised as king by many barons and foreign monarchs, such as the king of Scotland.

And in Norwich?

No sooner had the citizens waved goodbye to Louis and his Frenchmen, than the barons were wreaking havoc again. Half a century later the so-called 'disinherited' barons sacked much of the city. Having also been ransacked by another rebel force in the 1170s, the citizens had clearly had enough. In 1297, at their own expense, they began building the great city walls, parts of which survive to this day.

A little local difficulty: Norwich Cathedral was the scene of violence in 1272.

City versus Priory

In the summer of 1272 Norwich was in turmoil. The city's chief citizens were at war with the monks of the priory. By the time the dust had settled there were deaths on both sides, and the king had been forced to intervene.

How did it come to this?

The seeds of the disaster were sown in complex property rights, "complicated to the point of explosion" as historian James Campbell wrote in Medieval Norwich. After the building of the cathedral and monastery, founded in 1097 by Bishop Herbert de Losinga, the priory was the biggest landowner in and around the city. Like the nuns of nearby Carrow Priory, the monks' income of up to £2,500 a year was derived largely from their large estates in Norfolk. In some quarters this wealth was resented. The Normans had changed the shape of Norwich forever, building not only the cathedral and the castle, but also moving the city's main market from Tombland to its present position. Norwich was growing in size and prosperity. A charter granted by King Richard I in 1194 gave it formal city status. The city's burgesses (elected representatives) were mainly self-confident merchants unused to being pushed around.

What about the priory?

Tension between town and gown was nothing unusual. In Suffolk Bury St Edmunds abbey and citizens were also in dispute. Violence was to break out there, but not until 1327. Priories and abbeys maintained large staffs of servants, whose privileges and sometimes high-handed behaviour often made them unpopular, held vast estates and claimed jurisdiction over legal and property matters. It was important not only for prestige, but rents paid by tenants raised vital revenue. The Benedictine monks of Norwich had, by the late 1200s, held sway for the better part of two centuries, and were keenly aware of their position.

Storms brewing...

Disputes over jurisdiction and property rights rumbled on. In 1256 the priory's baker was killed in a dispute with a citizen. Because the death had occurred within the priory grounds the city bailiffs were denied the right to hold an inquest. This followed hard on the heels of a dispute a few years earlier in which the citizens had tried to enclose land within the prior's 'fee'. On that occasion a compromise was eventually reached, but the issue remained unresolved with both sides claiming to be in the right. When the city began building walls, inevitably it clashed both with the priory and people who lived outside Norwich, in such country areas as Taverham. The priory accused the city of encroaching on land belonging to it and the nuns of Carrow Priory, while country people were outraged that their age-old rights of way were being blocked by these uppity 'city slickers'.

This town ain't big enough for the both of us...

Tombland – the name means 'open space' – had long been the site of fairs and other public occasions. Its position right outside the cathedral gates brought citizens, priory servants and monks into close proximity. A bit too close, perhaps, with everyone in holiday mood and the ale and wine flowing freely. In June, 1272, the citizens were enjoying their customary recreations. These included targets for archery and lance practice. What happened next is unclear, as both sides later sought to exonerate themselves and incriminate the other. Later, the priory's case was put by one Bartholomew Cotton, whose Chronicle gave the monks' side, while the city's argument was put in a written work known as *Liber de Antiquis Legibus*. It appears trouble initially broke out with the priory servants, and in the ensuing melee a citizen was shot with a crossbow.

Time for a riot?

The city authorities arrested two servants after coroners had held an inquest. Angrily, Prior William de Brunham retaliated by excommunicating the citizens – a drastic and provocative step in a religious age, as it prevented them receiving Christian rites. By early August the priory was under siege. The prior stoked up the tension when he went to Yarmouth and returned with several boatloads of armed men keen to have it out with their city rivals. The Norwich men viewed the Yarmouth contingent as "evil-doers". Cotton claimed citizens climbed to the top of nearby St George Tombland Church and fired flaming arrows into the Close. The bell tower by the cathedral was gutted, along with St Ethelbert's Church just inside the gates. But the citizens said the monks started it, firing flaming arrows at buildings, and that the fire was self-inflicted. Those doing the fighting were not a 'mob' as we would understand it, but included some of the leading citizens, who believed they were being wronged. Their case was hampered by the subsequent looting of the church. Up to 13 priory defenders died, some executed formally, while others were imprisoned. But the monks and their allies hit back, the prior himself killing one attacker.

Someone had to intervene

King Edward I was not a man to tolerate such anarchy. His arrival in Norwich the following month ended the fighting. After hearing both sides, he appeared, on the surface, to side with the monks. The city was fined a massive 3,000 marks (about £2,000) and 29 people hanged out of 175 charged, which included some office-holders. Subsequent investigations also implicated de Brunham, who faced trial by his own bishops (they let him off). Within a decade though, Edward granted the city a new charter confirming some of the disputed property rights, thus giving with one hand what he took with another.

And the legacy of the violence?

If you take a look at St Ethelbert's Gate today you can see some pinkish-coloured cornerstones, effects of the fire. Trouble between city and priory was not over; during the Peasants Revolt of 1381 land disputes between citizens and the clergy broke into violence in many parts of the country, while in 1443 the so-called Gladman Rising in Norwich saw renewed conflict, though not as serious as that of 1272. Although relations between town and gown were not always so bad, many in Norwich were no doubt not unhappy to see the priory dissolved in 1538 by King Henry VIII during the Reformation. After that, the city of Norwich had no more competition over jurisdiction within the city walls.

13th century **1297**

Norfolk's defiant Earl

It took a brave man to say no to King Edward I. Yet that was just what Roger Bigod, Earl of Norfolk and the leading nobleman in East Anglia, did in January, 1297. Bigod lived to tell the tale – though some may argue that the monarch had the last laugh.

Risky business – defying the king!

Edward I, Hammer of the Scots and conqueror of the Welsh, was not a man to take no for an answer. So, when he demanded that the earls, magnates and great men of England join him in a war against France, he was less than pleased when many of them proved unenthusiastic. At a parliament in Salisbury, it was Roger Bigod who put into words what many of them were feeling. After he refused to join an expedition to reclaim lands in Gascony lost to the king of France, Edward lost his temper. "By God, Sir Earl, you shall go or hang," he told Bigod. "By God, O King, I will neither go nor hang," replied the Norfolk man. It was not the first time the proud and unbending Bigod family had fallen out with an English king.

They had 'form'?

The Bigod family had accompanied William the Conqueror, and fought at Hastings in 1066. Their reward was extensive land in East Anglia, followed by conferment of the title of earls of Norfolk. In Norfolk and Suffolk they built impressive castles, notably at Framlingham and Bungay. Granted the title of earls marshal of England, they were charged with raising and disciplining forces for defence of the realm, and were thus influential figures. The title reflected the importance of the wealthy counties of East Anglia at the time. But the Bigods often fell out with their kings. Most notably, Hugh Bigod, in the 1150s and 1170s, was at loggerheads with Henry II. In 1173 he joined a rebellion against the king, briefly occupied Norwich – and later had his lands confiscated. Another Bigod was a notable signatory to Magna Carta in 1215, curtailing the rights of King John, while another Roger Bigod and his brother Hugh were among the barons who seized power from Henry III in 1258. The brothers later rallied to the king's cause and helped defeat and kill Simon de Montfort, leader of the rebel barons, in 1265. For the next three decades the earls of Norfolk were mainstays of royal power. They held other lands in the strategically important Welsh Marches, then on the front line of English expansion, and in Ireland. In 1297, when King Edward I summoned

Stronghold: Framlingham Castle, a bastion of the Bigod Earls of Norfolk.

his nobles to Salisbury, he expected them to sail to Gascony and fight the French, while he invaded through Flanders in the north.

What went wrong?

Money was at the core of the argument. Medieval monarchs were not the all-powerful figures we may imagine. They relied on their powerful nobles for manpower and were always running out of money. Edward's funds were running low in 1297. In order to pay for his expensive wars he was squeezing his subjects dry to extract taxes. For example, in the 1290s, he tried to seize all the wool in the country as well as increasing taxes on landowners and the clergy. His conquests of Wales and Scotland and fruitless wars in France were bleeding the country dry. Mutterings were growing daily, though few dared publicly oppose a monarch described by a recent biographer as a "great and terrible king". Roger Bigod acted as the dissidents' spokesman. Calling on historical precedent, he refused to go to France unless the king led the army in person. All Edward's bullying and bluster could not shift him. Bigod left the parliament without permission, followed by his allies the earls of Arundel, Warwick and Hereford, to name a few.

Why was it important?

This defiance revived the constant spectre of rebellion that Edward's predecessors had faced. Although he attempted to seize Bigod's castles and manors in Norfolk and Suffolk, he was frustrated. For the first time in his 25 years as king, Edward began to look vulnerable. The wily monarch made some short-term concessions, masking the anger he felt towards the earls. At a meeting in Westminster, he declared he was acting in defence of England: "I am castle for you, wall and house," he declared. Many were won over, but Bigod and his supporters remained sceptical. Things could have escalated badly had not news reached England from the north. A common enemy united the nation. His name was William Wallace.

Braveheart!

Wallace was immortalised by Mel Gibson in his 1995 film. Great movie, very bad history. But it was correct in portraying English rule in Scotland as hated. Wallace defeated the English at the Battle of Stirling Bridge in September, 1297, moving into northern England and laying waste to it. Roger Bigod and the earls rallied to the king, galvanised by this threat from the Scots. They raised troops and joined a vast English army, 26,000 infantry and 3,000 cavalry strong, in an attack on Scotland. The Earl of Norfolk and his horsemen were in the vanguard of the force that comprehensively defeated the Scots at Falkirk the following year.

All friends now?

Neither Edward nor Roger had forgotten their falling out. Bigod feared the vengeance of the king, who had recovered from his weakness of the previous year, and was his usual powerful self. To head off royal displeasure the childless Bigod made the king his heir. It kept him out of trouble for the rest of his life. He was hopelessly in debt, not least because he had his private army to pay. For a generous annual annuity, he bought off Edward's hostility with this face-saving move. On his death in 1306 his property went to his widow, who followed him to the grave three years later. Edward himself died soon after Roger, but the property went to his successor as king, his son Edward II. So the monarchy had the last laugh in this stand-off with the last Bigod earl of Norfolk.

■ **Further reading: Edward I, A Great and Terrible King, by Marc Morris (2008)**

Fragments: The ruins of Greyfriars Monastery at Dunwich are a stark reminder of the days when this was an important medieval port.

The Dunwich storm

In 1328 the Suffolk port of Dunwich was one of the foremost towns in England. A place of merchants, sailors and priests, it had risen in importance for centuries. Then nature took a hand.

The city beneath the sea?

The name Dunwich means 'port in deep water' in old English. This was the basis of the town's foundation and prosperity. But the name took on a more sinister meaning from the end of the 13th century. Then a series of devastating storms instigated a long drawn out disaster, punctuated by dramatic episodes. Eventually the sea washed away almost the whole of the town, including churches, a market place and Dunwich's reason for being – its harbour. Buildings that were once a mile inland now stand precariously on the cliffs overlooking the shore. On a coastline that even today is notorious for its erosion, it serves as a warning of the power of nature.

What was there?

When the Christian missionary St Felix landed in England in about 630AD,

Dunwich was already a port, and probably had been since Roman times. It is referred to in the seventh century when the saint founded the first churches in the east of England. His see was centred at a place called 'Dommoc', which may have been at Dunwich, although it is just as likely to have been at the old Roman fortress at Walton Castle, or even at Felixstowe, to the south. What is not disputed is that Dunwich was a thriving place. Some unverified records describe it as being, at one time, the capital of independent East Anglia. Old maps suggest it had an ideal, sheltered harbour, around which everything else grew up. The town's heyday was yet to come. By the early Middle Ages, it was home to 3,000 people, and up to 18 churches, chapels and priories.

Where did the money come from to build them?
Dunwich was a centre for several different businesses. As England's fortunes rose with the wool trade, it became an export point for the finished woollens sent from this country to the Netherlands. Originating from nearby centres like Lavenham, the goods were shipped from Dunwich to Antwerp. Daring fishermen sailed as far as Iceland, possibly as early as the 11th century, bringing back herring. Local merchants grew rich on trade, so the money was available to build churches and houses. This was a place to reckon with. In 1173 the rebel Earl of Leicester tried to land troops at Dunwich to fight the king, Henry II. The citizens defied his intimidation, denying the invaders an anchorage. The town's women carried stones up to the men on the barricades, and the rebels backed off. As a reward the town was granted a charter 20 years later, making it a borough with rights to a degree of self-government. In the following century its proud freemen returned two MPs to Parliament. The town was also vital for defence of the realm. In 1242 Dunwich gathered a fleet of 80 ships prepared to go to war with the French. With its handy position at the top of a lowland cliff at the mouth of the wide Blyth estuary, it put Ipswich, then in an economic slump, firmly in the shade. For 13th century Dunwich folk, things couldn't have been going better.

Which is usually the cue for things to go horribly wrong. . .
In 1286 a storm swept part of the town into the sea, and partly silted up the Dunwich River. Apart from the devastation to property, this threatened the town's future, as it meant ships were hampered entering and leaving harbour. Undaunted, the citizens repaired the damage, building sea walls and constructing piers as windbreakers, and life went on. The real turning point came later. On January 14, 1328, ferocious winds whipped the sea up again. This time about 400 houses were destroyed and the market place flooded. The harbour was blocked, and trade switched to nearby Walberswick, leading to trouble between the two settlements. The very cliffs on which Dunwich stood, and which had been its fortune, now turned against it. The sand and gravel of which they were made

eroded away. The form of erosion known as 'longshore drift' had an irreversible long term effect. Dunwich was not alone. The harbours at Orford and Sole Bay to the south and north respectively also slowly disappeared. With the harbour went prosperity and the people, who began to abandon Dunwich after 1328. The churches and most of the houses were lost over centuries. All Saints' Church was the last to go over the edge in the last century.

Any survivors?

The only one to get away was the Franciscan 'Greyfriars' priory. Built in about 1230, it was abandoned to the sea in 1328, but rebuilt further inland, outside the original town. It may have escaped the sea, but it could not evade dissolution during the Reformation of the 16th century. Ominously, the cliffs are now just a few feet away from the surviving ruins. Although the town was depopulated, the descendants of the original freemen still had the right to vote for MPs, and there are tales of them taking boats out to sea and casting their votes where they thought the town hall had once stood! By the 18th century Dunwich was the most rotten of rotten boroughs. Despite having just eight inhabitants, it returned two members to Parliament. This abuse was not abolished until the 1832 Reform Act.

And today?

Dunwich is a beautiful, but haunting place. Tales of church bells being heard from beneath the waves are commonplace. The ghost writer M R James placed one of his chilling tales here, while fans of the science fiction author H P Lovecraft will recognise the sinister village of Dunwich, albeit moved across the Atlantic to Massachusetts. Recently, marine archaeologists have been hard at work at the bottom of the ocean trying to identify what little remains of Dunwich's drowned buildings. As this part of the coast is constantly threatened by erosion, perhaps it won't be the last place to disappear.

14th century **1349**

The plague years

"There is great death in Norwich, and in other borough towns in Norfolk, for I assure you that it is the most universal death that I ever knew in England."

Not another war?

Worse. Much, much worse. The plague. This letter of 1471 from Margaret Paston to her son in London illustrates the great fear of town dwellers for more than three centuries. Plague – the catchall term for the epidemic diseases that ravaged Europe. In 1348-9 the Black Death killed up to a quarter of the population of Europe. More than 25 million people are believed to have perished in this first, and most deadly, outbreak of bubonic plague. Within a year or so it disappeared only to break out again for the next 300 years.

What is bubonic plague?

It got its name from the painful, swollen lymph nodes, called buboes, which appeared on sufferers' bodies, frequently in the groin area. Dried blood under the skin turned black. After its onset death came to seven in 10 of those affected within two or three days. It was an awful death. Nobody knew what caused it. We think now that the infectious fever is caused by the bacillus *Yersinia pestis* transmitted to humans by the rat flea. At a time when people lived close to animals in unhygienic conditions, it was easy for the fleas to find a human host. Contemporaries blamed the plague on moral corruption, and looked for convenient scapegoats. It was thought too much exercise, too much sex or taking hot baths caused disease. Others thought it was spread by miasmas – poisons in the air.

What happened in East Anglia?

The first outbreak was on the south coast of England in August, 1348. It followed trade routes, spreading throughout the country. In Norwich they sought shelter behind their walls, but walls do not keep rats out. The 18th century historian Francis Blomefield reported that it reached the city on January 1, 1349. No accurate records were kept of how many people died. Blomefield calculated it at 57,304 people, but that seems far too high a figure. Recent estimates indicate that out of a population which may have been as high as 25,000 in 1348 as few as 6,000 survived, or were still living in the city, 20 years later. Two thirds of the clergy died and only one in three market stalls were occupied the next year. The dead were piled high in carts and buried in communal pits in Cathedral Close. Others were buried in nearby St George Tombland churchyard. It is said the graveyards there had to be raised to cram in the bodies. In Lynn almost half the population died in 1349. Yarmouth was devastated. In its crowded Rows two thirds of the population perished, and construction of the town's walls stalled for lack of workers. Economic life ground to a standstill, and some people abandoned their families when they became contaminated. Work abruptly stopped at Norwich cathedral cloisters on June 25, 1349, according to ecclesiastical records, and did not restart until 1355.

But life went on. . .

Eventually the country recovered, though the reduction in population had a long term impact, and the psychological scars must have been deep indeed. Plague returned with varying virulence. People tended to lump bubonic plague in with other epidemics, such as the mysterious sweating sickness that claimed lives in the 1530s, typhus, smallpox, syphilis and all the other nasty ways you could die. Later outbreaks tended to hit towns and ports most severely, so places like Norwich, Yarmouth, Ipswich and Lynn were at risk. Poorer areas with the worst sanitation suffered, prompting the authorities to clamp down, blaming poverty for disease. The plague returned every 10 years or so until the next great outbreak. In 1578 Norwich celebrated the visit of Queen Elizabeth I. She had stayed in the city along with an entourage some 2,000 strong. Soon after their departure that September, the worst plague epidemic since the 1340s arrived. This time there were officially 4,800 victims in Norwich, though the real number could have been twice that. The old pits were re-opened for mass burials. This time the city authorities, including mayor Augustine Steward, ordered that contaminated houses should be isolated. They were locked and bolted from the outside, windows boarded up and red crosses painted on the doors. Sometimes the occupants survived. Most of the time the bodies were left until bailiffs had found somewhere for them to be buried. In one episode people in quarantined houses turned to cannibalism. The ghost of a young woman said to appear in Tombland is apparently that of a 1578 victim.

Some cheerful news please. . .

Well. . . you were a bit safer in the countryside. Richer people were able to leave town when the plague struck. The only thing that seemed to stop it was a destructive fire. Gradually people made the connection between overcrowded towns, dirty conditions and disease. Norwich suffered again in 1603 and 1625 so, when news of plague in London reached Norfolk in September, 1665, everyone held their breath. Ships from Yarmouth were turned away from the city walls, but the death toll grew. By the time it subsided in 1667 nearly 3,000 people had died. This was the last outbreak of this plague in Britain. It disappeared as mysteriously as it arrived.

14th century **1381**

The Peasants' Revolt

South of North Walsham, on the Norwich road, stand three weathered stone crosses. They mark the spot where East Anglia's Peasants' Revolt came to a bloody end in 1381.

The revolt was in London, wasn't it?

While Wat Tyler and the men of Kent and Essex were storming London, in Norfolk and Suffolk similar mayhem ensued. It was put down thanks to a ferocious fighting bishop. The Norfolk revolt is largely a tale of two men; Henry Dispenser and Geoffrey Lister.

Why were they revolting?

The traditional story of the 1381 rising is of a downtrodden peasantry finally standing up for themselves, only to be cut down by the aristocracy. While the view that the final straw was a hated poll tax is still regarded as true, things were not quite so simple as we thought. For one thing, not all the rebels were peasants, illiterate serfs and tillers of the land. Many were part of the village 'elite' – craftsmen and artisans. Geoffrey Lister (or Litester) for example was described as a North Walsham dyer. Conditions had been improving for the

Bloody cross: The fighting Bishop of Norwich erected stone crosses to mark the place where he defeated the rebels in 1381.

common people since the depopulation caused by the Black Death of 1348-9. With fewer workers for hire, they could command higher wages, and move around more freely. An example of a family who benefited was the Pastons. Clement Paston was a Norfolk landworker in the late 14th century who was able to buy land and raise his family to wealth and nobility within a few generations. Feudalism was dying – but was not quite dead.

Nobody had told the aristos?

Some historians think the revolt was a result of frustration that things were not changing quickly enough. Although there was an element of rudimentary socialism in renegade priest John Ball's famous slogan 'when Adam delve [dug] and Eve span, who was then the gentleman?' we don't know what most of the rebels felt. A source of discontent was land ownership; during the rising land deeds were a prime target of rebels' wrath. Attempts to curb wages exacerbated the situation. We know little about Lister, but plenty about his nemesis, the Bishop of Norwich. Henry Dispenser was nobility through and through. The youngest of five brothers, he was no gentle priest. This trained soldier had fought in Italy and Scotland by the time the Pope appointed him a bishop. Aged about 38 in 1381, he was a hard, argumentative man – "unbridled and insolent", according to St Albans chronicler Thomas Walsingham.

Ripe for rebellion...

As news of the rising in the south-east spread, East Anglia was also affected. From the north Norfolk village of Felmingham came the 'king of the commons'. Geoffrey Lister was a businessman and property owner. The rebels he led were intent on destroying property records, usually held by religious institutions. These were considered unfair, their destruction an expression of natural justice. Property rolls at priories like Binham were seized and burnt. Then the rebels marched on Norwich. Their motives are hard to gauge, as few survived to voice them after the revolt was suppressed. They were joined by some gentlemen, such as Sir Roger Bacon, of Baconsthorpe, who attacked Yarmouth.

Did nobody oppose them?

On June 17, two days after Wat Tyler's death at Smithfield, Norwich opened its gates to Lister's rebels, massed on Mousehold Heath above the city. Why? Did he have sympathisers within the walls, was it out of fear of the consequences, a loss of nerve among the ruling class with no clear direction from central authority? Young King Richard had given the London rebels certain reassurances, and this acted as a 'green light' for action. Lister seized the castle and forced four captured knights to serve him at table. The church was again targeted. The nuns of Carrow had to hand over their substantial property deeds, which were burnt. Prisoners were taken from the gentry, while members of the judiciary were singled out for vengeance. Looting and extortion continued for a week.

What happened in Suffolk?

In Bury St Edmunds a mysterious figure called John Wrawe was among the prominent rebels. Described as a former chaplain from Sudbury, he led up to 400 men to Bury St Edmunds. There the authority of the abbey was much resented, and Prior John de Cambridge was among those beheaded, along with Sir John Cavendish, a hated lawyer and owner of Overhall manor, while prisoners were released from the abbey jail. Many of the rebels felt they had some form of legal authority for their actions. In Ipswich lawyers, particularly those associated with the poll tax, were targets. Wrawe was among those later arrested and sentenced to death following a trial in London.

Enough was enough

One man took matters into his own hands. Bishop Dispenser was in Lincolnshire when trouble broke out; unlike many around him he kept his head. With a small force, he rode east dealing out instant retribution to those he apprehended. Dealing with rebels in Bury St Edmunds, he reached Norwich on June 24. By then the mood had changed. The ruling class, buoyed by the withdrawal of the rebels from London, regained their nerve. Promises made by the king were torn up. It was time for revenge. Lister's rebels withdrew towards North Walsham. The bishop's army caught up with them south of the town. The rebels, many of them bowmen, barricaded themselves behind wagons and carts, but were overrun. Perhaps their morale had dipped by then.

Time for some quick hangings...

Witnesses said the bishop let many of the rank and file go, but made an example of the leaders. Some tried to seek sanctuary in a nearby church but, as it was not yet sanctified, Dispenser had them executed. Lister initially escaped, but was soon captured. Accounts differ as to what happened next. Some said the bishop dragged him off to be beheaded, while others said he first heard his confession, absolved him, then walked with him to his place of death. Either way, the game was up for the man once hailed as "the idol of Norfolk". His quarters were sent to Norwich, Lynn, Yarmouth and to his home village "so that rebels, and those that rise above their place, may learn how they will end".

What's there now?

Bishop Henry erected three crosses to mark the event, one of which can be seen just off the Norwich Road. They are marked on Ordnance Survey Map Norfolk Coast East Explorer 252.

15th century **1459**

The funeral of Sir John Fastolf

St Benets Abbey had never looked better. Late in 1459, Norfolk's great and good gathered in their hundreds, all the monks spick and span amid a feast fit for royalty. It was Sir John Fastolf's final farewell.

A one-way journey

This Norfolk knight, veteran of The Hundred Years War and supposed inspiration for Shakespeare's comic character, died on November 5, 1459. His death, and splendid funeral, were the closing of one chapter and the opening of another. Closely tied up with a saga of legal, and then violent, repercussions was Norfolk lawyer and landowner John Paston.

Fastolf – drinking pal of Prince Hal, wasn't he?

Shakespeare employed a lot of artistic licence in his character of the cowardly, dissolute Falstaf in Henry IV Parts I and II. The real Sir John Fastolf was a far more distinguished character. Born in Caister, near Yarmouth, in about 1378, he came from an established Norfolk family. Fastolf made his name in the French wars, fighting at Agincourt in 1415. As a close ally of the king's brother, the Duke of Bedford, he was in the right place for lucrative promotions. His marriage to a wealthy widow some years his senior, Millicent Scrope, also brought land and wealth to his growing portfolio. Returning to England, he was a rich man, with land in East Anglia and a fine house in Southwark, London.

And John Paston?

The Paston family, from north Norfolk, rose from obscurity via land and the law. John Paston divided his time between London and Norfolk, while his loyal wife Margaret supervised their difficult affairs at home. We know a lot about the family because they wrote a series of letters, which have been an invaluable source of information to historians. Both Fastolf and Paston were involved in serious disputes over land and money – and this drew them together. During the later 1440s, Paston, then in his thirties, befriended the ageing Fastolf. As the old knight's wife had died, and he was childless, the issue of to whom he was to leave his money became a vexed question. In the mid-1450s Fastolf, now in his seventies, moved back to Norfolk. He had come to trust and like John Paston almost as a son – he was the only person Fastolf really trusted.

Easy-going sort of chap?

Fastolf was notorious for his bad temper. A man who saw issues in black and white, he made life increasingly hard for his loyal servants. Having at one time relied heavily on his secretary William Worcester and chaplain Thomas Howes, he now entrusted his affairs to John Paston. Fastolf was keen to ensure his legacy lived on in Norfolk. He proposed setting up a college to train priests at Caister. There he had inherited land and built a castle. Fastolf wanted to found the college with an annual endowment of £200. But that needed a royal licence, which was not always easy to obtain without legal knowledge. Fastolf knew his time was nearly up. His friend Paston was most likely to achieve his aims, secure his lasting fame on earth and ensure his estates were not broken up. Why not make him sole heir, rather than have the legacy dissolved among distant relatives or other claimants? Although Fastolf drew up a will in the summer of 1459, that November he was on his deathbed at Caister. At his side was John Paston, to whom he dictated a new will – leaving the lawyer everything.

Sounds fishy!

Easy to be cynical and assume foul play. But Paston was an honest man, albeit, in the words of historian Helen Castor "practical and unsentimental". He was fond of Fastolf, who had earlier written to him, saying: "I feel well that I was never beholden so much to any kinsman of mine as I am to you." Whatever people thought of the last-minute will, Fastolf was given a magnificent funeral at St Benets Abbey. It's now a ruin, but it must have been quite an occasion. There, in the abbey on the banks of the River Bure, it was fitting that Fastolf was laid to rest. He had paid for rebuilding of a new aisle on the south side of the chancel, at a cost of £616, while much of his fortune in gold, some £2,600, was deposited at the abbey. Craftsmen had painted 18 banners and more than 50 pennants bearing Fastolf's coat of arms and family heraldry. Mourners wore the finest black gowns – black was then the most expensive clothing. John Paston attended with his family and an impressively large following; as did his long-time friend Judge William Yelverton. Soon afterwards, Paston left for London to attend the probate hearing.

A matter of routine?

It did not take long for trouble to start. Yelverton, a friend of Fastolf's and an ally of the Pastons, was among the first to cry foul – probably at the funeral itself. As a judge in King's Bench he was an influential man. Fastolf's servants, including

Remains: The ruins of St Benets Abbey, where Sir John Fastolf was buried, now have a windmill built within them.

Worcester and Howes, were also upset, as was the knight's family. All felt snubbed by the changed will; all were suspicious of Paston's actions. Although the Paston family inherited Fastolf's estate, they had little time to enjoy it. The following spring an inquest at Buckenham declared the true heir was an obscure nephew of Fastolf's. The case might have stayed in the law courts to drag on for years – a kind of medieval Bleak House – but at a national level civil war was about to break out. The houses of York and Lancaster began their contest for the crown, known now as the Wars of the Roses. At local level law and order broke down. The Duke of Norfolk turned greedy eyes on Caister Castle. A decade after Fastolf's death, and three years after John's death, the Paston family were besieged there. They were forced to surrender the castle, although they later won it back.

And what of Fastolf's legacy?

His plan for a college at Caister was abandoned as his posthumous affairs became so entangled. His tomb at St Benets was a victim, like the abbey itself, of the Reformation. When the abbey was dissolved in the 1530s much of its stone was carried off to be used for buildings in Norwich and elsewhere. All that remains is a gatehouse, with a later windmill constructed incongruously within it. The site is a landmark of the Norfolk Broads, immortalised by artists. Like Sir John Fastolf, it has not been forgotten.

■ **Further reading: Blood and Roses, Helen Castor (2004)**

15th century **1475**

Lynn's Common Market

In 1475 Europe's first 'common market' was thriving – and Lynn in Norfolk was at its heart.

Some kind of early European Union?

The Hanseatic League was an international trading organisation loosely united in one great endeavour – making money. In 1475 Bishop's Lynn – as the town was then known – became the site of a permanent base for the traders from Germany and further afield. It marked Lynn out as an international port of the first order.

Go east, young man!

It's probably best to realign our view of the map. Instead of looking south towards London from west Norfolk, or west and north towards the rest of Britain, look due east. There, in a line, are Lynn's trading partners – the German cities of Cologne, Bremen, Hamburg, Lubeck, Stralsund, Wismar and Rostock, further on the Polish city of Danzig, then further to the north-east Riga, now in Estonia, Novgorod, in Russia, and the Swedish island of Visby. They sound a long way off, but to the merchants of Lynn in medieval times they were in fact close to hand. The Hanseatic League was founded in about 1259. In an era of weak central government, and little sense of nationalism, these city states felt the need to stick together and protect their trading interests from thieving pirates and greedy monarchs. League members shared the perils of travel and difficulties of dealing with rapacious overlords and their tax demands. With its base in Lubeck, north-west Germany, the League soon had its own armed fleet of ships in and around the North Sea and Baltic waters. It also began to throw its weight around, forcing some governments to allow free passage and favourable trade concessions for its members. The League's cities were powerful and wealthy, many acting as bankers; England's King Edward III had his crown jewels pawned to a Cologne moneylender. The Hanse was not entirely popular, but its influence was growing.

What about Lynn?

The north-west Norfolk port and town was thriving in the Middle Ages. Since the Bishop of Norwich, Herbert Losinga, had taken it under his wing in the early 1100s – and given it its prefix – Lynn had dominated its immediate hinterland. Goods from the interior – wool cloth and salt – arrived in Lynn from the towns and villages of East Anglia. Like Norwich and Yarmouth, it looked to the east. German merchants from the Baltic and beyond needed trading partners in England. They arrived in London, Hull, Boston and Bishop's Lynn. In 1271 they were granted trading privileges in the town, confirmed after some disputes 40 years later. German traders were regular visitors to summer fairs, selling fish, timber, wax, iron and pitch for shipbuilding in return for wool, salt, skins and lead. In return Lynn men sailed east, particularly to Danzig and Stralsund. It took another century before the Norfolk traders had permanent bases overseas, but by the 1380s they had a significant presence in Danzig. Margery Kempe was a Lynn woman living at the time. Later famous as a businesswoman and traveller, her son married a Prussian girl from Danzig (now Gdansk) in the 1420s. There was two-way traffic; German shoemakers lived in Lynn at this time.

Everybody getting along fine then?

Trade disputes were frequent, with privateers preying on shipping. The Hanse ganged up on England following raids on shipping. After several years of war at sea, King Edward IV made concessions, as he needed help in his invasion of France. He signed the Treaty of Utrecht in 1474, giving the Hanse properties in English ports. While in London they built a kontor – a cross between a warehouse and a dormitory for travelling traders – at what was known as the Steelyard, in Lynn they had their own building near St Margaret's Church. This was built in 1475, and still stands. It is the only remaining medieval Hanse warehouse in England. When built it had its own quay. The Hanse's buildings were often targets of popular discontent, as many resented the foreigners' privileges.

The League's days were numbered

Discovery of the New World in 1492 switched the focus of world trade to the west, while the rise of powerful nation states and local commercial competitors undermined its autonomy. Tudor King Henry VIII and his successors were in no mood to allow unregulated trade in England, particularly if the profits were going offshore. In 1537 Bishop's Lynn became King's Lynn. It was good news for the town's merchants, who took control of their affairs without ecclesiastical interference. International trade continued, but the Hanse merchants were no more. The League was all but extinguished during the 16th century. In Lynn, the old kontor was sold in 1751 to a local man named Edward Everard for £800. He added an elegant looking dwelling, known as St Margaret's House, to the warehouse. After 20th century renovation this became Lynn's register office, owned by Norfolk County Council. Lynn's Hanseatic links were recalled recently with a festival, the highlight of which was the arrival of a replica ship, the Lisa Von Lubeck. King's Lynn rejoined the Hanse, a modern organisation aiming to recreate the spirit of trading links between the League's original members.

16th century **1529**

The last guildhall

In the 1520s the merchant princes of Lavenham began work on their most magnificent building yet. Times were good in this industrial town – but its days were already numbered.

Industrial? Lavenham?

Quaint and picturesque, this picture postcard tourist attraction full of timbered houses set in calm Suffolk countryside seems the very opposite of industrial. That's how it is today. But back in the 15th and early 16th centuries, this was the 14th richest town in England. It was home to reputedly the wealthiest commoner in the land. It was to Tudor England what Bradford or Manchester became to the early Victorians.

And it was all down to wool!

"I thank God and ever shall
It was the sheep that paid for it all."

So wrote one wealthy English clothier. Woollen cloth was medieval England's greatest export. It is estimated that in 1300 there were 15 million sheep in the country, outnumbering people by more than three to one. The big money was made in processing the raw material into fine cloth and exporting it to the continent. Cloth went from the coast to the Low Countries, usually via ports like Antwerp. By the later Middle Ages the importance of wool to the economy was reflected in the 'Woolsack', the stuffed seat that the Lord Chancellor sat on in the House of Lords.

Why did Lavenham do so well?

Sheep were grazed in the countryside around the town, but much of the wool was brought in from wide open grazing country in north Lincolnshire. There the hardy Lincoln Longwool sheep produced superb wool. Lavenham and other neighbouring towns, such as Long Melford and Sudbury, had a number of things in their favour. They had a supply of water, needed in the finishing process, and an abundant supply of labour. Relative proximity to the coast also helped. The real boom time was the 1400s. In this era the enterprising clothiers built bigger and better houses to show off their wealth. They rebuilt the town's church, the magnificent St Peter and St Paul.

Boom town: The guildhall of Corpus Christi in Lavenham was built in 1529.

What work went on?

Raw wool needed a lot of work to turn it into luxury cloth, and a lot of people were involved. From sorting, carding, spinning, washing, dyeing, weaving, fulling, tentering and finishing, Lavenham and surrounding villages were humming with industry. It was noisy, mucky labour, and people worked in shifts. Fullers, for example, had one of the least attractive jobs in the land. They had to walk up and down in huge vats of stale urine. The ammonia created soft cloth by drawing the grease from the wool. Then there was dyeing. Lavenham was famed for its blue broadcloth. Dyes came from plants; for blue, the plant woad was used. Madder, on the other hand, was used to create red dye. The wool was dyed before weaving; hence the phrase "dyed in the wool". Imagine the smell, all mixed up with human waste and butchers at work. There were no sewers in the town, so everything went down the middle of the street.

Where there's muck. . .

. . .there's money. Surviving wills show how much wealth was made from trade. The Spring family in particular thrived. In 1523 clothier Thomas Spring III left in his will 26 manors and property in 100 others. He also paid for a wonderful private chapel in the church. Merchants banded themselves into guilds. These were less trade bodies than social and religious institutions. Members paid a subscription, and could borrow from a central fund and draw a pension in hard times. Each guild held celebrations on religious holidays, putting on plays and conducting processions. Lavenham had five, though there were more than 500 in Suffolk. These existed throughout the country, though few of their buildings survive. Another fine example can be seen at King's Lynn, that of St George. This predates the guildhall of Corpus Christi at Lavenham. Little is known of the guild of Corpus Christi. It seems to have had fewer members than that of Lavenham's Saints Peter and Paul, which had its own priest as early as 1446, but it may have been more exclusive – for the merchant elite. The Corpus Christi guildhall was built to impress from the outside. Inside, it was plain, with no heating, a ground floor meeting room and upper floors perhaps used as warehouses. Carpenters used green and unseasoned timber, and prefabricated every frame before constructing the building within a few days. Today it is reckoned one of the finest timber-framed buildings in Britain. In 1529 it proclaimed that its members were part of a flourishing industry.

But times were changing. . .

Lavenham Guildhall was built between 1520 and 1529, just as the good times were ending. The government of the day, then as now, couldn't see working people without taxing them heavily. That's what Henry VIII did in 1524, and his "harsh and universal" taxes along with restrictive regulations hit hard. Riots broke out in protest at Lavenham, with up to 4,000 people on the streets. Lord Chancellor Cardinal Wolsey, himself a Suffolk man, intervened, and John Spring helped break up the trouble. By this time the richest merchants had moved out of town, building country houses and joining the gentry. In 1578 Sir William Spring was Sheriff of Suffolk, and helped escort Elizabeth I on her East Anglian progress that year. Lavenham was lagging by then. Continental wars cut off trade with the Netherlands, while Flemish workers introduced new practices which undermined Lavenham's products. Its dependance on a single industry became its weakness. By the 1620s bankruptcies and unemployment were rife. Hard times for the workers.

Cloud with a silver lining?

The town's misfortune then is its good fortune now. Trade decline meant it slumbered as a backwater for centuries. Those buildings that survived were left largely untouched. When the guilds were suppressed at the Reformation in the 1540s the guildhall became parish property. It was subsequently used as a jail, workhouse, almshouse and warehouse. Wartime evacuees were received there in 1939 and it later became a British Restaurant. The National Trust took it over in 1951.

16th century **1539**

The Binham whitewash

In about 1500 craftsmen finished a work of art in a north Norfolk church. Less than half a century later others deliberately wiped it off the face of the earth. Both groups believed they were doing God's work.

Burning issues. . .

Binham Priory and St Mary and the Holy Church stand in a quiet village near the coast. The priory and church had shared the same space since the 12th century. As the 16th century dawned few would have predicted the Catholic church would soon be replaced in England by Protestantism. The priory was home to monks and was lavishly illustrated with colourful imagery and icons – as was the parish church. Historian Simon Schama visited Binham during filming of his televised History of Britain, and spoke of "the ardent, coloured noisy world" of Catholic England. At the centre of this riot for the senses was a stunning rood screen.

What is a rood screen?

The rood screen was the division between the chancel and the nave in any church. At Binham it showed a painted array of saints who would have been recognisable by the items they carried – for example St Catherine of Alexandria is seen with the wheel on which she was said to have been martyred – as well as a representation of the king and Jesus Christ. The rood itself at Binham was a statue of Christ on the cross, with the Virgin Mary on one side and St John on the other. It was raised aloft centrally on a beam above the screen to be seen by the whole congregation, who would crane their necks upwards to appreciate the scene. On top of the screen was a walkway called a rood loft, reached by a set of spiral stairs, which can still be seen in the south wall of the church. The loft was used by the priest as a platform from which to read the Gospel at Mass, and also by the choir, who would stand on the loft to sing psalms and hymns. Candles placed above the rood beam would have added to the spiritual atmosphere. Historians reckon the screen was created between 1471 and 1500; a painting of King Henry VI, who lived from 1422 to 1471 helps to date it. It is believed to have been the creation of two of Binham's monks.

Very nice – but not for everyone

Reformers hated this imagery. They believed it distracted people from true religion. All this paraphernalia, plus the central role of the priest ministering to his illiterate flock in clerical Latin they couldn't understand, was anathema to the growing number of Protestants. Theirs was a religion based on preaching sermons and close study of the Bible – in English. To them illustrating the saints on the rood screen was superstitious idolatry. Worshipping saints was like bowing down to graven images – and didn't the Bible forbid that? Items like rood screens created a barrier between God and His people, and should be removed. Your immortal soul depended on getting this right. They wanted to replace the worship of images with that of the word of God. In this case they took that literally.

Enter Henry VIII. . .

In the 1530s Henry and his chief minister Thomas Cromwell attacked the monasteries. A rebellion broke out in the north to protect traditional religion. The brutal and bloody suppression of this Pilgrimage of Grace in 1537 encouraged the rest of the country to obey the king's orders. Two years later, when Binham Priory surrendered to the crown, its treasures were confiscated, the bells melted down and its stone gradually carted away. The parish church next door survived, but did not escape the reformers. Archbishop Thomas Cranmer's English Bible was placed in every church and read to the people. In 1539 Binham's rood screen was whitewashed over. Gone were the colourful saints; in their place were overpainted written texts from this new Bible. Over the picture of Christ went a quotation from I Timothy 6; 10-12, *For coveteousness of money is the roote of all evyll.* What went through the minds of the men doing this job? Were they reforming zealots, Puritans abolishing superstitious nonsense – or ordinary craftsmen just doing their job and scared of the king's laws. We'll never know, but the visual shock for those heading into church to worship must have been palpable. Similar scenes were acted out at churches across England. The reforms of the late 1530s were the beginning of a confusing period in which the country switched to Protestantism, back to Catholicism, and then – definitively – to Protestantism under Elizabeth I. Churches and their interiors were on the front line in this struggle, and it was not to be concluded for over a century. Work by historians such as Eamon Duffy have suggested most ordinary people favoured traditional religion until well into Elizabeth's reign.

No more saints then?

For centuries the rood screen was a ruin. Norwich artist John Sell Cotman painted the church in 1809 showing it still obscured by the whitewash of 1539. But gradually, something strange happened. The whitewash began to flake away, and the faces of the saints began to reappear, faintly, peering almost furtively through the writing. Close examination of the screen has identified a number of characters, though not everyone agrees with this list; Michael the Archangel, Saints Catherine, Roche, Mary Magdalene, Barbara, Helena (with fragments of the true cross),

Return of the saint: St Michael reappears as the whitewash flakes away, and the image peeps through the Bible text.

Apollonia, Alban, Zita and Sebastian, along with Henry VI and Jesus. Many of us would struggle to identify the lesser saints, but Christians in the 16th century would have recognised them easily. Saints were as familiar as household items to them from the stories they heard in church and from their families.

■ Four of the original six panels, each with four saints, survive. You can see them at Binham Priory, near Holt. The building is in the care of English Heritage, and open to the public. Tel: 01328 830362.
www.english-heritage.org.uk/
■ Further reading: The Stripping of the Altars, Eamon Duffy

Mary's game of thrones

In 1553 East Anglia decided who would rule England.

It is early July. The gentry of Norfolk and Suffolk have gathered, along with their followers and thousands of ordinary people. Flags and banners flying, they wait outside Framlingham Castle in Suffolk. Once the home of the dukes of Norfolk, this dramatically sited fortress is now the property of the crown, although it has seen better days. The atmosphere is expectant. These people know an army is marching from London against them, led by a proven soldier who only four years earlier had bloodily repressed a rebellion in Norwich. The woman who rides out on a white horse to review the men ready to fight for her is the one they believe should be queen of England – Mary Tudor, 37-year-old daughter of Henry VIII.

A combustible political situation?

England in July, 1553, was a country on the brink of civil war. The death of the young King Edward, whose government had introduced hugely controversial religious and economic reform, had sparked a crisis. In London a new queen had been crowned. Teenage Lady Jane Grey's claim to the throne, as great-niece of Henry VIII, had been pushed by her scheming father-in-law. John Dudley, Duke of Northumberland, the power behind the boy king's throne, had married her to his son Guilford. Four days after the king's death, on July 6, he altered the succession to make Jane queen. At the heart of this coup was a mixture of dynastic intrigue and religious conviction. Northumberland, his family and allies were determined Protestants, as well as ambitious and ruthless. In 1549 he had led an army partly composed of foreign mercenaries to Norfolk to crush Robert Kett's peasant rising.

What about Mary?

Mary Tudor was the eldest child of Henry VIII, daughter of Catherine of Aragon. She was Catholic, and thus the choice of conservatives throughout England. Her life had not been easy. After the death of her beloved mother, she was made illegitimate, then restored to legitimacy after the execution of Anne Boleyn. But she was not allowed to freely practise her devout Catholicism. This merely made her more determined to return England to what she saw as the true faith.

Time for action. . .

Mary was at Hunsdon Hall in Hertfordshire when Edward died. Her life would

Rallying point: Mary Tudor gathered her followers at Framlingham in Suffolk in the summer of 1553.
Illustration: Annette Hudson

surely be in danger from Northumberland. Summoned to London following her brother's death, she instead fled to Sawston Hall, near Cambridge. Owner John Huddleston, a loyal Catholic, disguised her as a dairy maid and smuggled her away. Northumberland's supporters burnt the hall down in revenge. Mary next made for Kenninghall, in Norfolk. This was the main seat of Thomas Howard, Duke of Norfolk, leader of the conservative faction at court. He was at the time imprisoned, but his people provided a warm welcome for the Tudor princess. From Kenninghall she issued a rallying call to her subjects by letter and word of mouth to come to her support. Perhaps she had been waiting for this moment, and had a network of followers in place.

What was Northumberland doing?
In London, the duke assembled a formidable looking 1,500-strong army and marched towards Cambridge. In this moment of high drama, Mary's supporters persuaded her to leave Kenninghall and make for the more easily defended bastion at Framlingham. Quick to rally round was Sir Henry Bedingfeld, from Oxburgh Hall, west Norfolk. He provided Mary with 140 armed cavalry. With her flag flying from the castle word spread, and soon thousands of followers were camping in the deer park below the castle. As they were joined by many of the local nobility, with their armed retainers, it was clear Mary's position was getting stronger.

Why did so many people support her?
The magic of the Tudor name, natural conservatism, outrage at the upstart Dudleys' seizure of the crown, a feeling religious reform had gone too far and fear of civil war loomed large. Many Protestants preferred a legitimate Tudor heir to Northumberland's coup. While her father was feared as well as respected, she also benefited from her mother's lasting popularity among ordinary people. Mary's actions and demeanour helped her; she acted like a queen and looked like one. Reviewing her followers, with tears in her eyes, she declared "it was God's work". Conservative East Anglia was convinced. Northumberland's support disintegrated. At Yarmouth the royal fleet mutinied. This was largely down to Sir Henry Jermingham, one of Mary's supporters from Hellesdon, near Norwich. According to one account, he rowed out to the ships, which were sheltering in the harbour to avoid bad weather, and appealed to the sailors. Convinced by his arguments, and crying 'Long live our Queen Mary', they threatened to throw their officers overboard. The navy's defection prevented Northumberland from receiving help from overseas. Not only that, the sailors marched inland along with some of the heavy cannons from their ships, and joined the forces at Framlingham. Meanwhile, London had also declared for Mary, and most of Northumberland's army deserted as he headed north. The Earl of Arundel, a powerful magnate, arrived at Framlingham to confirm Mary as queen. On July 20, unopposed, she issued her first royal orders from the castle, and rode in triumph to London.

What happened next?
Jane had abdicated on July 19. Her 'reign' had lasted nine days. Northumberland surrendered, and was quickly executed. Mary – reluctantly – had Jane beheaded the following year, fearing she would be a focus for future risings. During her reign she tried to reverse the Protestant revolution. English history would have been radically different had Mary lived longer and had a Catholic heir; as it was she died childless in 1558. Her Protestant half-sister Elizabeth inherited the crown. Sawston Hall was rebuilt when Mary was queen, partly at her expense.

16th century **1556**

Hardley Cross

Landmark: Hardley Cross marks the place where Norwich and Great Yarmouth's jurisdictions met.

At the point where the Rivers Yare and Chet meet stands a stone cross. It marks the spot where, four and a half centuries ago, it was decided where Norwich and Yarmouth's jurisdiction lay.

A landmark boundary. . .

Today the Norfolk Broads are a beauty spot. Thousands of tourists are drawn to the area each year by the appeal of this unique landscape. But, up to the dawn of the 20th century, since medieval times and before, it had been a trade highway. It was Norfolk's window on the outer world at a time when water transport was vital. Poor road links between East Anglia and the rest of the country meant water was an easier way to get people and goods around. Up until the 19th century it was quicker to get to the Netherlands from Norfolk than it was to travel to London. As international trade grew, and government at local and national level became more sophisticated, so did the need to regulate it. So, in 1556, the city of Norwich was granted a charter by Queen Mary and her husband, King Philip of Spain. It decreed that the spot where the writ of Norwich ran out, and that of Yarmouth began, should be at Hardley Cross. The only reminder of that time is the solitary cross that has stood at the crossroads of the rivers for centuries.

What was the charter about?

The charter, granted on April 3, 1556, set the limits and boundaries of the city of Norwich and the county. "From the Wensum, which river was formerly granted to the city, by the outward part of the bank of the river to Trowse bridge. . ." and so on, encompassing Harford, Cringleford, Hellesdon, Horsham St Faith, Little Mousehold, Thorpe and Heigham, many of which had been separate hamlets. "And by the same water eastwards, including the whole water to Hardley Cross and so returning, taking in the whole river Wensum." The city's corporation was given the right to "perambulate" the bounds yearly. This gave rise to an annual ceremony held at Hardley Cross. There officials from Norwich and Yarmouth, presumably arriving by boat, would conduct the 'Hardley Inquest', at which they would declare all the 'abuses and privileges' related to trade issues on the Yare.

Why all the song and dance?

Norwich had been growing throughout the medieval period. A succession of royal charters gave it increased powers. Despite violent upheavals in 1272 and 1443, which incurred royal displeasure, Norwich was on the rise. In 1403 a charter granted by Henry IV gave it effective self-government. From then on it had the right to elect a mayor, a sheriff and bailiffs, who became important people with a great deal of responsibility. The citizens often clashed with the cathedral monks and nuns of Carrow Priory over land ownership and legal issues. That changed following the Reformation, when the city took over what had previously belonged to religious houses. Meanwhile, relations with Yarmouth were not always cordial, despite the close trading links. Back in 1272, the cathedral monks and Norwich citizens had been in violent dispute. The abbot had sent for reinforcements to Yarmouth, who arrived by river and took part in melees with the Norwich men. A more commercial dispute broke out in 1331. In that year the king fixed staples for wool, sheepskins and other commodities, "none of which were to be sold anywhere but in a staple town. Norwich was the only one appointed in Norfolk and Suffolk. This provoked the burgesses of Yarmouth.. . they stopped all ships, vessels and boats coming through their port to the city". It took the intervention of the monarch, and a threat to confiscate the Yarmouth men's goods, to end the matter.

What kind of trade?

The earliest vessels plying the route between Norwich and Yarmouth were known as keels. They carried wool products, which were the source of England's medieval wealth. Norwich was famous for its weavers, a trade that flourished until the early 19th century. By the 13th century a specific Norwich cloth called worsted was popular abroad. The wool was exported from East Anglia's ports to customers on the continent; places such as Antwerp and Bruges were vital. Imports included such items as sea coal, Swedish iron, Baltic wood, onions and herrings. Merchants set up large warehouses along the River Wensum in Norwich to store goods; such a place is Dragon Hall in the city's King Street, which has been restored and opened to the public. Immigrant workers from France and the Netherlands settled here as the good times continued. The Dutch in particular influenced Norfolk; we see many examples of Dutch gables on buildings in Yarmouth and Norwich, and elsewhere in the county. Later on, wherries, large cargo-carrying barges, became familiar sights on the river, and they enjoyed their best days in the 1800s. The rise of the railways and improved road links towards the end of the 19th century spelt the end for river trade, and the subsequent rise of tourism. Today, the wherry remains an emblematic image of the Broads.

What's at Hardley Cross?

A familiar landmark to boaters, it stands at a crossroads. The Yare leads in one direction towards Yarmouth, in the other to Norwich, while a turn takes you to the River Chet, and the villages of Chedgrave and Loddon. Keen walkers can revel in a wonderful trek along part of the Wherryman's Way. This is a 35-mile recreational route following the old trading route along the river. If you start out from Loddon, it's about five miles to the cross, and the route – on easy footpaths – takes you past the waters of Hardley Flood, a hidden gem teeming with wildlife. If you make it to Hardley Cross, take a look at the Latin inscription carved on it. Our Latin is a bit rusty, but it tells us the cross was repaired in 1820, "in the time of Thomas Hickering, sword-bearer of the City of Norwich". The sword-bearer (armigeri) was an official in the city corporation, something in keeping with the role of the cross in establishing civic rights and duties. Echoes of this particular role live on in the annual Lord Mayor's Parade held each July in Norwich, in a figure carrying a sword who goes before the mayor. The role was one of those formalised in the city's charters, such as that granted by Queen Mary in 1556.

16th century **1577**

Attack of the Black Dog

In August, 1577, the Devil came down to Suffolk, and got loose in Bungay and Blythburgh. In the guise of a giant, black dog. So the legend goes.

A hell hound with red eyes and fiery breath, perhaps?
That's him. Over the centuries there have been many sightings throughout East Anglia of such a beast. He goes under the name Black Shuck, of which more later. The incidents at two Suffolk churches are the best documented versions of this persistent tale.

Sounds like a 'shaggy dog' story!
On Sunday, August 5, 1577, a terrible storm was underway. At St Mary's Church, Bungay, as vicar Robert Belye was conducting the Sunday service, people quailed from the "darkness, rain, hail, thunder and lightning as was never seen the like," (according to a contemporary pamphlet writer). Many were praying for relief from the elements. Suddenly, without warning, the great dog burst through the doors. According to one ryhme:
All down the church in midst of fire, the hellish monster flew
And, passing onward to the quire, he many people slew
The dog began clawing and biting people. The Rev Abraham Fleming wrote later:
"This black dog, or the divel in such a likenesse (God hee knoweth al who worketh all,) runing all along down the body of the church with great swiftnesse, and incredible haste, among the people, in a visible fourm and shape, passed between two persons, as they were kneeling, and occupied in prayer as it seemed, wrung the necks of them bothe at one instant clene backward, in so much that even at a moment where they kneeled, they strangely dyed."
After that it ran off. But its bloodthirsty attack was not over. Running 12 miles eastwards to the coast, the dog arrived at Blythburgh Church, causing the steeple to collapse. It "cleft the door, and returning to the steeple rent the timber, brake the chimes and fled". Two people died at Bungay, and a man of 40 and a 15-year-old boy were killed "stark dead" at Blythburgh.

A good yarn, but what's the truth?
The Elizabethans were quick to see the hand of the Devil in all mishaps. At this time everything from crops failing, beer going flat or the illness of a child were put

Dog day: The weather vane in Bungay recalls the day the devil hound is said to have run amok in the town in 1577.

down to witchcraft or demonic intervention, so it may be that in the aftermath of the storm, this story grew in the telling. Some versions of the Blythburgh story do not mention a dog, merely the Devil ripping through the church during the storm. The logical, rational explanation is that it was the storm which did the damage; at Bungay, sure enough, two people died, but it seems they were in the belfry when it was hit by lightning. This is mentioned in a churchwarden's book, though no official mention was made of casualties. At Blythburgh, the Devil's scorch marks were later recognised etched onto the great north door. As for what really caused this, we may never know. At Bungay, a great fire in March, 1688, damaged the church so badly it needed extensive rebuilding and any evidence of Black Shuck or any other Satanic agent was destroyed.

So, that's it then; a bad storm and some superstitious locals?
In Bungay there were good reasons to fear a spectral hound. They went back to the

12th century when Hugh Bigod was Earl of Norfolk; a proud, restless man, known as Hugh the Bold, he rebelled against King Henry II. He built a castle at Bungay in the 1160s. In 1173 his bid to take Norwich was thwarted, and he fell back to Bungay. There all his boasts proved of no avail; he was forced to surrender to Henry. The king fined him heavily and demolished his castles. Bungay Castle survived, though Hugh had to pay a further fine to avoid its destruction. The keep was 90ft high, the walls 18ft thick – and it overlooked St Mary's Church. Hugh later died on crusade in Syria. But the story goes that he returns to Bungay in the shape of a devil dog and, still angry at having to pay fines to the king, revenges himself on the unwary.

What about this Black Dog?

The tradition of Black Shuck goes back to Anglo-Saxon or Viking times. Historians believe the name dates back to these times, as do sightings of the dog. His appearances are held in some parts to presage death or disaster of some kind. His name may derive from the Anglo-Saxon word scucca meaning 'demon', or possibly from the local dialect word shucky meaning 'shaggy' or 'hairy'. Sometimes Black Shuck has appeared headless, and at other times he appears to float on a carpet of mist. According to folklore, the spectre often haunts graveyards, sideroads, crossroads and dark forests. Black Shuck is also said to haunt Beeston Bump, a hill close to Beeston Regis and Sheringham.

And in Bungay?

The Black Dog tale caught the local imagination. The hound is immortalised by a weather vane in Bungay market place depicting a dog with a streak of lightning, alluding to the 1577 apparition. He is incorporated into the town's coat of arms as well as on several buildings, while organisations such as the town's football and running clubs have adopted the nickname. St Mary's underwent further misfortune. In 1644 Puritan iconoclasts – those who hated religious imagery – smashed stained glass and icons under Parliamentary commissioner William Dowsing. Today it is disused, though still consecrated ground and looked after by the Churches Conservation Trust. Holy Trinity Blythburgh, in its lofty spot on the Blyth estuary, is known as the Cathedral of the Marshes.

Anything else?

In the 1890s Sir Arthur Conan Doyle was holidaying in Cromer when he heard the Black Shuck legend. Apparently it inspired him to write the classic Sherlock Holmes tale, The Hound of the Baskervilles. Cromer Hall was the model for the home on the moors where the tale was set.

16th century **1578**

A Royal Progress

***"I have laid up in my breast such good will as I shall never forget in Norwich"*. So said Queen Elizabeth I on her one and only visit to Norfolk.**

Ah, a royal visit. All that pomp and circumstance. . .

The Queen's summer 1578 Progress was a grand affair. Accompanied by a vast train of courtiers, soldiers and servants, Elizabeth I left Greenwich in mid-July, spending two months on the road. Her week-long stay in Norwich in August was the highlight of the tour. It was marked by sumptuous pageants and feasts, and honours bestowed on the chosen few. Behind the scenes was a feat of organisation, with court officers scouring the countryside for weeks in advance for suitable accommodation, disruption to the government of the country, uncomfortable lodgings for many of those accompanying the monarch – and a hefty bill for the Queen's hosts to pick up after she had gone.

What was the point of it?

In an age of personal monarchy, it was important for the Queen to be seen by her subjects. It

Good Queen Bess: Elizabeth I toured East Anglia in the summer of 1578.

lent the monarchy prestige, and helped impress people by her presence. During her reign she spent many summers on progress, though she never strayed too far north or west. Until 1578, 20 years into her reign, she had not been to East Anglia. It may have held unpleasant connotations. After all, at Framlingham in 1553 her half-sister Mary claimed the throne, while the county was dominated by her awkward Catholic cousins, the Howard family – Dukes of Norfolk. Only six years earlier the fourth duke had been executed for treason after conspiring with Mary Queen of Scots, so family gatherings were never easy affairs. Religion divided the country; with the external threat from Catholic Europe, 'recusants' who refused to go to Church of England services were persecuted. Many lived in Norfolk.

Surely, East Anglia was loyal

Many of the gentry had benefited greatly from the sale of former monastic land. They had a stake in the Tudor monarchy and supported Elizabeth against Catholicism. The temper of the common people was harder to judge, though most were patriotic. The suspicious Elizabethan regime could never be sure. It was with an air of caution that the Royal Progress set out. Gentlemen ushers, the harbingers of the procession, preceded it, giving towns and cities along the route an approximate itinerary. A court official named Thomas Churchyard was in Norwich. It was his job to organise festivities for the Queen's arrival, one which he tackled with enthusiasm, and left a written account giving us details of the Progress. Following weeks of preparation, on July 11 the Queen set out. With her came the Yeomen of the Guard, 130 strong, and the mounted Gentlemen Pensioners. The Queen's council came too, including her trusted Chancellor Lord Burghley, her favourite the Earl of Leicester and her spymaster Sir Francis Walsingham. Others joined the procession later, including ambassadors from France and Scotland, as the whole government of England took to the road. Many humbler folk accompanied; in all, it is thought 200 to 300 carts rumbled along the poor quality roads, with hundreds of people on horseback and on foot.

North up the M11 then?

Roughly following the route of modern roads, the Progress reached Audley End, Essex, on July 26. This was one of many Howard properties in the area, and it may have been with mixed feelings that the young heir, Philip Howard, met the Queen. She later stayed at his Norwich mansion – Surrey House. The prestige he gained from hosting the monarch may have made the cost worthwhile; the same could be said for most of the other hosts along the route. At the Suffolk border Elizabeth was met by the assembled gentry in their finery, a display matched when she later entered Norfolk. She stayed at Melford Hall, near Sudbury, as well as former monastic property at Bury. Reaching Norfolk on August 11 the Progress stopped at Kenninghall, another palace owned by the executed Duke of Norfolk. Following a stop at Bracon Ash, it was on to Norwich.

A grand entrance?

The stay in Norwich from August 16-22 was the high point of the Progress. At considerable expense the city had been tidied up; muckhills were moved, streets gravelled and widened, smelly animal waste from butchery taken beyond the walls (along with the more unsightly beggars, no doubt). The city's musicians – The Waits – wore smart new uniforms. They had even been paid in advance, a rare luxury. City children had been recruited by Thomas Churchyard to take part in pageants rich in classical and mythical analogy, according to the fashion of the time. This was the sight which greeted the Queen as she entered Norwich through the freshly decorated St Stephen's Gate. From there she pressed through the welcoming crowds to the cathedral and on to the Bishop's Palace, her base for the week.

A packed itinerary?

The best that Norwich could offer was put on. Elizabeth also went hunting in Costessey deer park, owned by the Catholic Lady Jerningham. Going back through St Benet's Gate into Norwich – greeted by another of Churchyard's pageants – the Queen paused by the Dutch church. There the preacher who attended to the spiritual needs of the Dutch and Walloon migrant textile workers recently arrived in Norfolk presented her with an expensive cup. (She was clearly impressed; after returning to London she sent money back to aid poor foreign workers). The following day it was across the river up the hill to Surrey House (modern St Leonards Street). Going back into the city the preacher at the Great Hospital recited lines in Latin, to which the queen is said to have listened intently. Sadly, Churchyard's elaborate pageant involving waternymphs was ruined by a sudden thunderstorm. There was a torchlit boat tour along the river, during which Elizabeth passed by what is probably the city's oldest pub, the Adam and Eve. We don't know if she had time to pop in for a drink! After knighting five gentlemen, the Queen left Norwich on Friday, never to return.

Anything else?

After the Queen left, a number of local Catholic recusants were tried in Norwich, and fined. They included Edward Rookwood, whose Suffolk house the Progress had stopped at earlier. Shortly after that plague broke out in Norwich; many blamed the Progress for spreading it. A royal visit was a mixed blessing.

17th century **1605**

Frozen in time

In 1605 work was well underway on a grand summer house for an important family. Then history took a hand, the work stopped – and Lyveden New Bield was frozen in time.

An intriguing building

You can see it from a distance amid beautiful rolling countryside west of Peterborough, near the town of Oundle. A mysterious, roofless, floorless and windowless construction with an air of abandoned grandeur which asks more questions than it answers. The tale of Lyveden New Bield, and why it was never finished, is caught up in the tragic tale of religious strife of 16th and 17th century English history, culminating in the Gunpowder Plot of 1605. At its heart is a fervent Catholic gentleman named Sir Thomas Tresham.

Local bigwig?

The Treshams were the most important people in this part of Northamptonshire. Since the reign of Henry V in the 1400s they had profited from their control of rich mineral deposits and valuable hunting grounds of the ancient Rockingham forest. Like many of the rising gentry class who came to prominence under the Tudor monarchs, they became even richer from enclosing land for sheep farming. This was the most profitable industry in 16th century England; income from wool exports to the continent funded lavish lifestyles among the elite. By the late 16th century Tresham received a whopping £1,000 per year in rent from farming tenants, and a similar sum from the sheep business. Born in 1544, Thomas inherited the estates of Lyveden and Rushton aged 15 on the death of his grandfather during the first year of Elizabeth I's reign. The Treshams moved in the highest circles of court; fashionable and well-educated, Thomas was friendly with William Cecil, the queen's first minister, and Lord Chancellor Christopher Hatton, who helped arrange prestigious and lucrative government posts for the family. Thomas was knighted by the queen at Kenilworth in 1575.

Where did it all go wrong?

Tresham led a life of conspicuous consumption, spending freely on friends and family. Four of his six daughters, for example, were married in expensive weddings to peers or future peers. He may have got away with this profligacy, but what really undid him was religion. The Treshams were devout Catholics, not a

Mysterious: Lyveden New Bield was never completed.

good thing to be as England swung towards Protestantism under Elizabeth. Tresham's wife, Muriel Throckmorton, was the daughter of another wealthy Catholic family, from Warwickshire. By the 1580s, with England menaced by Catholic Spain and Mary, Queen of Scots, attracting Catholic support as a potential rival to Elizabeth, views hardened. Religious non-conformity was punished by fines and exclusion from government posts. Tresham paid penalties for not attending Church of England services (recusancy) totalling £8,000. For a quarter of a century he was periodically imprisoned during periods of political crisis, such as when the Spanish Armada threatened in 1588. His wealth never recovered.

Why not convert?

Like the Bedingfelds of Oxburgh Hall in Norfolk, it seems never to have occurred to the uncompromising Treshams to blow with the wind. The accession of James VI of Scotland and I of England in 1603 gave Catholics new hope. Thomas Tresham had created Rushton Triangular Lodge in the 1590s, an extraordinary construction which demonstrates his Catholicism. The number three, symbolising the Holy Trinity, is everywhere. Despite his debts, Tresham was still a wealthy man. In about 1604 he started on a new house at Lyveden. It was known as the 'New Bield' to differentiate it from the nearby 'Old Bield', the family's main seat dating from the 1450s, of which little remains. The New Bield seems to have been designed to imitate St Peter's in Rome. It is meant to symbolise the Passion of Christ. Symmetrical in the shape of a Greek cross, it has four equal arms stretching out from the centre. Religious inscriptions line the outside walls, including the phrase 'Gaude Mate Maria' (Rejoice Mother Mary). Apparently, when the sun shines through the parlour window in the morning, it casts a shadow of a crucifix against the wall behind. This religious iconography was to "delight and edify the beholder," wrote Tresham.

Who was going to live there?

It seems to have been a secondary residence for Sir Thomas. The house had a great hall and parlour on the first floor and a kitchen and buttery in the basement. It may have been meant for use as a "Secret House" or summer garden/hunting lodge where he could relax for a short while, probably while the main house was being spring cleaned, and enjoy his faith in private. Tresham took a keen interest in the building. Family letters include one he sent from Ely prison directing his foreman on the laying out of the garden and bowling alley at Lyveden. He had big plans for the New Bield. It was not to be. Events conspired against the Treshams. On September 11, 1605, Sir Thomas died, leaving debts of £11,000. His elder son Francis inherited. He, like his father, was Catholic. He was mixed up with a dangerous conspiracy. His cousins Thomas Wintour and Robert Catesby, angered by continued state oppression of Catholics, decided to assassinate King James at the opening of Parliament. A chap named Guy Fawkes was also involved. . .

Gunpowder, treason and plot. . .

It seems a letter, written by Francis to a friend warning him not to go to the opening of Parliament, alerted the authorities to the plot. In the crackdown that followed, Francis was arrested. Accused of treason, he died in the Tower of London one month later, probably saving him from being executed. Younger brother Lewis inherited, but it was his mother Lady Tresham who repaid her husband's debts, offsetting the final £1,000 by selling sheep, corn and hay at Lyveden before her death in 1615. All work stopped at the New Bield, which remained an empty shell. A period of cost-cutting may have safeguarded the family's future, but Lewis spent lavishly. His son William, who died childless in 1643, was the last of the main line of Treshams.

And the New Bield?

It looks as if the builders have knocked off for lunch. No roof was ever built, windows were left scored for their intended glazing, walls were left bare and tablets of stone stayed blank without inscriptions. Frozen in time alright, but how the building has survived 400 years untouched is a mystery. In 1922 it was donated to the National Trust. In recent years the abandoned secret garden has been unearthed and restored – a rare survival of Elizabethan garden design.

■ **Lyveden New Bield is south-west of Oundle. nationaltrust.org.uk**

17th century **1637**

Samuel Lincoln and the New World

In April, 1637, a 15-year-old boy left his native Norfolk for a new life. Samuel Lincoln's descendants would go on to make history, but he was not alone in leaving 17th century East Anglia to live the American dream.

And what was wrong with Norfolk?

Samuel Lincoln was born in 1622, and was baptised at St Andrew's Church, Hingham. His family were poor, though this appears to have stemmed from a family dispute that resulted in his father Edward being disinherited by his grandfather, a wealthy landowner from nearby Swanton Morley. At Hingham, the congregation was led by a Puritan priest. Puritans wished to rid the Church of England of its remaining Catholic vestiges, but by the 1630s their cause appeared to have received a fatal blow. Charles I appointed William Laud as Archbishop of Canterbury, and he reversed recent trends by reviving what many felt to be Catholic symbolism; screens between priest and congregation the chief of many concerns. With the Bishop of Norwich, Matthew Wren, a leading anti-Puritan persecutor, to many the New World across the Atlantic appeared a better option than staying in England.

Although many stayed in the liberal Netherlands temporarily, they wished to mould a new society of their own. Even Oliver Cromwell, then a fenland farmer of Puritan beliefs, contemplated leaving these

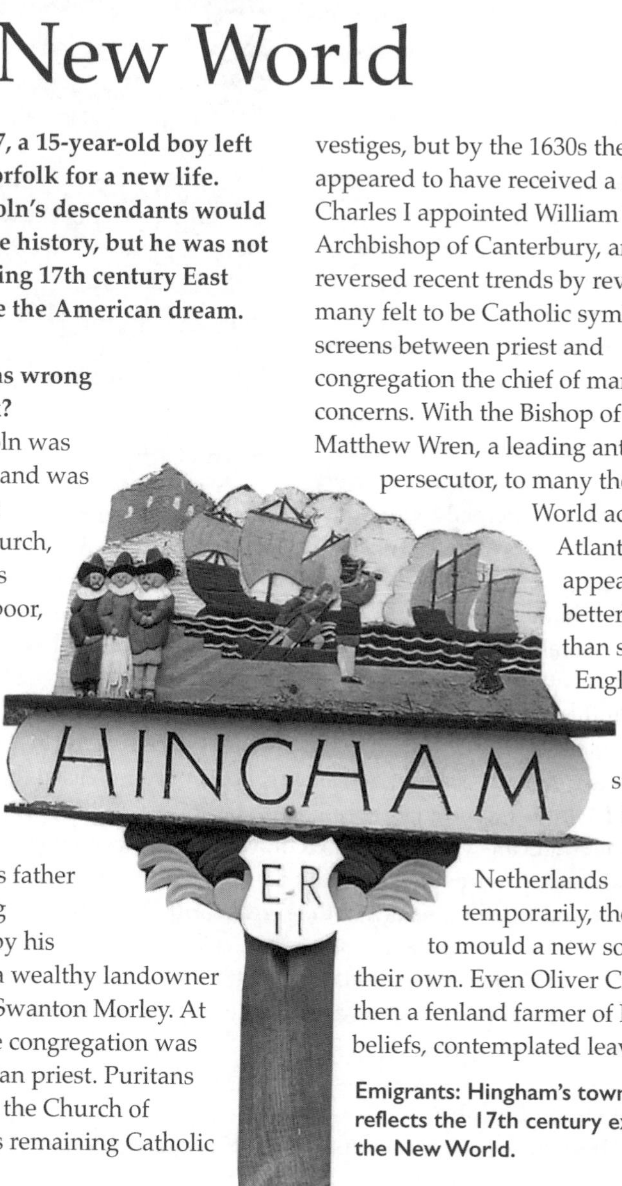

Emigrants: Hingham's town sign reflects the 17th century exodus to the New World.

shores during the 1630s. In the increasingly poisonous atmosphere of pre-Civil War England it was a decision many took as a way of following their religious convictions. There were other considerations. Over-population squeezed scant resources, and fierce Poor Laws oppressed humble people. During the 1630s more than 20,000 English emigrated to Massachusetts alone.

Memorial: This display in St Andrew's Church, Hingham, celebrates the Norfolk town's links to Abraham Lincoln via a young man who emigrated in 1637.

Why Massachusetts?

It was a welcoming haven for disillusioned Puritans. In 1620 a group of religious dissenters, now known as the Pilgrim Fathers, had landed in Plymouth Bay and formed a colony. A decade later wealthy Suffolk landowner John Winthrop also sailed for North America at the head of a group of colonists. A convinced religious reformer and a very determined man, he helped found the state of Massachusetts as a godly republic. This was a different colony to a place such as Virginia, which had been founded as a commercial venture and attracted an altogether different type of colonist. Democratic and free-thinking it was not, but it was a place where Puritans could safely practise their religion. "We shall be as a city on the hill," declared Winthrop. Music to the ears of such as the Revs Robert Peck and Peter Hobart, vicars of St Andrew's, Hingham. Peck, described by the historian Francis Blomefield, as a man of "violent, schismatical spirit" antagonised the Anglican authorities. He lowered the chancel railing of the church, in line with the Puritan belief that the Anglican church was too removed from its congregation. This may sound trivial – but it was a huge issue at the time – and Peck faced losing his living. He decided to lead his flock to the New World. Fellow Cambridge graduate Hobart, also a Hingham native, joined him. Emigration was not an easy option. The emigrants "sold their possessions for half their value," according to one account. Town clerk Daniel Cushing also left, along with his father Matthew, in 1638.

What about young Lincoln?

Samuel had been raised a member of this Puritan congregation. By 1637 he was

Left: What is the real meaning of the ancient depictions of the Green Man? This superb example can be found in the cloisters of Norwich Cathedral. Story on Page 15.

Below: The mysterious Iron Age 'hill fort' at Stonea Camp in the fens, reputedly stormed by the Romans.
Story on Page 18.
Illustration: Dr Ben Robinson

Above: Ealdorman Brithnoth went down fighting against the Vikings at the Battle of Maldon in Essex. This statue is on the promenade there. Story on Page 27.
Picture: visitessex

Left: Henry VIII's daughter Mary played a deadly 'game of thrones' at Framlingham in Suffolk in July, 1553. Story on Page 64.
Illustration: Annette Hudson

Hardley Cross stands where the Chet and Yare rivers meet. It marked the division between the jurisdictions of Norwich and Great Yarmouth in Tudor times. Story on Page 67.

Above: Melford Hall is a quiet, picturesque spot now, but as civil war broke out in 1642 it was the scene of a riot. **Story on Page 82.**

Left: Queen Elizabeth I conducted a Royal Progress through East Anglia in the summer of 1578. **Story on Page 73.**

Illustration: Annette Hudson

Radical firebrand Thomas Paine was born in the Norfolk town of Thetford in 1737. His statue was put up in the town in 1964. Story on Page 111.

The mighty walls of Burgh Castle, near Great Yarmouth, have stood since the days of the Romans. Story on Page 21.

Above: Bank House on the North Brink in Wisbech was home to the Peckover banking dynasty. Story on Page 133.

Left: King Charles II loved horseracing at Newmarket, and rode a winner there in 1675. Story on Page 97.

Illustration: Annette Hudson

Above: The Desert Rats trained for the Normandy D-Day landings in 1944 at a base in Thetford Forest. Replica Cromwell tank Little Audrey stands at the entrance to the site. Story on Page 153.

Left: The town sign at Hingham shows a group of emigrants waiting to sail for America. In 1637 a youth named Samuel Lincoln made the journey. His descendant was Abraham Lincoln, President of the USA. Story on Page 79.

Above: Saint Michael peers through the Biblical text as the Binham rood screen reappears centuries after its whitewashing during the religious reforms of the 1530s. Story on Page 61.

Below: The view from West Lynn to King's Lynn seen today. Parliamentary gunners would have surveyed a similar scene during the 1643 Civil War siege. Story on Page 88.

apprenticed to a weaver of Norwich, called Francis Lawes. In April of that year he joined Mr Lawes and his family by embarking on a ship called The John and Dorothy. They arrived in Boston, Massachusetts, after a hard voyage of just under two months. Samuel settled in a place which had been founded just four years earlier, originally called Bare Cove, south of Boston. He must have felt at home, for the town had been newly christened . . . Hingham. People from the Norfolk town were already there, including his own elder brother Thomas, who helped set him up with land. Samuel Lincoln went on to marry, and his descendants achieved greatness in America. His Puritan beliefs are reflected in the names of his 11 children; Biblical names such as Samuel, Levi and Abraham dominated. He died in 1690, after helping establish the new town; he was among the people who built the first church there. His great-great great-great grandson Abraham became the 16th President of the USA in 1861. Through the furnace of the American Civil War, he ended up freeing the slaves, and made himself the reputation as one of that country's greatest leaders. Clearly the Lincolns cut their links with the mother country fairly quickly, and perhaps their dissenting roots influenced their political decisions. Other leading Lincolns included Benjamin Lincoln, Secretary of War and one of George Washington's generals in the War of Independence (known as 'the Revolution' in the USA), and Levi Lincoln, Sr, another revolutionary, and his son Levi Lincoln, Jr, each of whom became governor of Massachusetts. Maine governor Enoch Lincoln was another descendant. Another Hingham family who left Norfolk in the 1630s were the Gilmans. Edward Gilman's descendant Nicholas was the New Hampshire delegate who signed the US Constitution during the War of Independence.

What happened back home?

In Hingham, Norfolk, the exodus of many of its brightest and best – a 17th century 'brain drain' – hit hard. The town petitioned Parliament for help, claiming to have been devastated by the loss of its leading citizens. These days the American connection is maintained in mutual regard. In 1919 a bust of Abraham Lincoln was placed in the church in a ceremony attended by the US ambassador of the time. Part of the inscription reads: "In this parish for many generations lived the Lincolns. . . citizens of the US have erected this memorial in the hope that for all ages between that land and this land and all the lands there shall be malice towards none with charity for all." The town sign at Hingham depicts a group waiting for a ship on a quay, memory of a time when emigration seemed the best option for many Norfolk people.

17th century **1642**

The Melford mob

In the summer of 1642 England descended into civil war and chaos. At one family home in Suffolk, mob violence and religious intolerance broke out. The story has a tragic ending.

Pretty place, picturesque village. . .

Melford Hall is peaceful and serene today. This was not the case in the mid-17th century. This Tudor-built, mellow looking red brick mansion, next to the large village green in Long Melford, near Bury St Edmunds, had thrived for over a century. It had hosted Queen Elizabeth I and 2,000 courtiers in 1578, and its deer park was the pride and joy of its first post-Reformation owner, Sir William Cordell. Although a man of humble origins he had risen in the world of the law, and bought the estate, which had once been the property of the monks of St Edmundsbury. He was a Roman Catholic, and was to be the last of this religion to hold the post of Speaker of the House of Commons until Michael Martin came to hold the role in the first decade of the 21st century. His successors, although disbarred from holding high office in the government because of their religion, thrived both at court in London and on their Suffolk estate.

But times were hard for Catholics

Resentment and suspicion among the Protestant majority grew in the early years of the 17th century. The Spanish Armada and the Gunpowder Plot made things worse. High profile Catholics were subject to occasional persecution. But, by the time Sir Thomas Savage took possession of Melford Hall after the death of his grandmother, their prospects were improving. The Stuart kings, James I and Charles I were more sympathetic to Catholicism. An early protege of the influential Duke of Buckingham, Savage married in 1602. Unusually among wealthy families at the time, he married for love. His bride was Elizabeth Darcy, the daughter of Thomas Darcy, third Baron Darcy of St Osyth Priory, Essex. Like her husband, she was a Catholic. It was a happy marriage, and the couple had a phenomenal 11 sons and eight daughters. While Sir Thomas was Chancellor of the Household of Queen Henrietta Maria, wife of Charles I, Elizabeth was a lady of the bedchamber. Hopefully she stored up happy memories, as her later life was pretty miserable.

Stately: Picturesque Melford Hall was the scene of mob violence and drunken escapades as civil war broke out in the summer of 1642.

Storm clouds gathering. . .

Henrietta Maria was an ostentatious French Catholic. English Puritans hated her with a vengeance – and all those associated with her. Trouble was stored up during the 1630s. Sir Thomas died in 1635 and his son John inherited his estates. His mother was created Countess Rivers. This could not disguise the uncomfortable fact the family were bankrupt. A programme of improvements to the house, partly to accommodate their massive family, and complete refurnishing of the rooms, along with extensions and glorious tapestries, strained the finances to breaking point. In the cellars there were reportedly 2,887 gallons of beer – of which more later. By 1635 the family were £14,000 in debt, and had to mortgage the estate.

And not popular with the neighbours

Throughout 1642 Charles I's situation had been deteriorating. Driven from London, he began raising forces in the north and west, where the Royalists were in the ascendancy. The country was divided. Although many people wanted no part of the fighting, extremists on both sides held sway. In an atmosphere of uncertainty and growing lawlessness, Puritan-dominated Parliamant began to crack down on suspected Royalists. Houses were searched, people arrested and property confiscated. Catholics were particular targets, with several priests lynched by mobs. For Countess Rivers, then aged 61 and living at her family home in Essex, the bad times were just beginning. That summer, with real news in short supply, local Parliamentarians were taking the law into their own hands. East

Anglia, especially this part of Suffolk, was Puritan country. In Cambridge an attempt by university colleges to send valuable metal plate to the king to be turned into weapons was thwarted when a local landowner called Oliver Cromwell seized the town. Puritan mobs invaded churches and smashed religious images.

Time for a sharp exit

On August 22 Charles raised his standard at Nottingham, declaring war on Parliament. That same day the Colchester house of the Catholic Lucas family was ransacked. Their neighbour, Countess Rivers' property at St Osyth, was also attacked. Avoiding the rioters, the countess fled to what she hoped was sanctuary at Melford. But the Puritans pursued her and, joined by locals, turned on the hall. A contemporary diarist wrote: "All glass was broken, all iron pulled out, all household stuff gone, all ceilings rent down or spoiled, all likely places where money might be hidden dug up, the gardens defaced, beer and wine consumed to knee deep in the cellar, the deer killed. . ." The countess escaped, pausing, it is said, to throw some pearls in a nearby pond.

At least things couldn't get worse!

Her tenants refused to pay rent, Parliament fined her and her son, and Puritan troops invaded the hall again the following year. At least they didn't confiscate the estate. After a period of exile in France, on her return to England in 1650 she was arrested for debt. Imprisoned in a debtors' prison in London she died the following year. Her son was also arrested, and had to sell Melford and its nearly-ruined hall for £29,000. It took several generations and a great deal of money to restore Melford to its former glory. Almost exactly three centuries after the attack on the hall, a potentially even more serious disaster occurred. In February, 1942, the hall was used to billet troops during the Second World War. A fire broke out in a sealed room, gutting the whole north wing and destroying other parts of the house along with priceless treasures. It was lovingly reconstructed after the war with the help of a local architect. Today, it is a popular tourist attraction set in a lovely part of Suffolk, and hosts many events.

■ **Melford Hall passed to the National Trust in 1960, but remains a family home.**
Tel: 01787 379228.
nationaltrust.org.uk

17th century **1642**

Oliver's army

"I had rather a plain, russet-coated captain that knows what he fights for, and loves what he knows, than that which you call a gentleman and is nothing else." **Thus Oliver Cromwell described the kind of soldier he wanted under his command. Many of them he hand-picked from his neighbours.**

Fen tigers?

On August 29, 1642, Cromwell set up his headquarters at the Falcon Tavern, in the centre of Huntingdon. He was raising a troop of cavalry, about 100 men, to fight for Parliament in the looming civil war against the Royalists of Charles I. Cromwell wasn't looking for any old recruit – the sort who joined up for plunder or liquor. He wanted a new kind of soldier, one that fought with a sword in one hand and a Bible in the other. But he also wanted a practical man – who praised the Lord and kept his powder dry. In sober, hard-working East Anglia there were plenty of candidates.

Why Huntingdon?

Cromwell had been born there in 1599, raised and educated in the town. He had been the town's MP in the ill-fated Parliament of 1628. Although a member of the minor gentry, and a farmer by occupation, his family links and political convictions led him into opposition to the king. It served him ill in the short-term. When Charles dismissed Parliament, Cromwell lost his seat, and was virtually hounded out of town by his opponents. Moving his young family to nearby St Ives saw him go down the social scale, but his fortunes improved when he inherited valuable property at Ely. But his inclination towards religious and political radicalism hardened. In the 1630s he became a convinced Puritan, a critic of the Archbishop of Canterbury's policies. Closer to home he opposed the imposition of the unpopular tax known as Ship Money, and also took up the cause of dispossessed fenmen. The 1630s saw the start of fen drainage. Investors known as adventurers began turning the wetlands into fertile farmland, but commoners – the Fen Tigers – lost out. Cromwell, now living at Ely, became their spokesman.

Big fish in a small pool?

By the summer of 1642 he was well known locally, though not yet a national figure. Elected to Parliament as MP for Cambridge two years earlier, he was an ally of Parliamentarians John Pym and John Hampden. As England drifted towards civil war, there was no doubt whose side Cromwell would take. His first decisive intervention came when the authorities at Cambridge University decided to send valuable metal plate to the king. Cromwell was having none of that. Gathering support among friends and family, there was a showdown on the Great North Road, and he confiscated the plate. He then seized the magazine at Cambridge castle and ordered guards to be placed on bridges there and at Lynn. On August 22, Charles raised his standard at Nottingham. War was inevitable.

Gather the troops!

Cromwell first drew on support from his kin. His brothers-in-law John Desborough and Valentine Walton were with him, also his son, 19-year-old Oliver. At Huntingdon, Cromwell called on the fenlanders to take up arms for "the freedom of the gospel and the laws of the land". Most of the men who joined were of the "middling sort", freemen and their sons, yeoman farmers of solid and

Ironside: Oliver Cromwell raised troops for Parliament in Huntingdon in the summer of 1642.

dependable stock. Although Cromwell, then in his early forties, had never been in battle, as a farmer he knew horses. Their procurement, training and maintenance were a passion for him. The horses used during the civil war unlike the Arab and Barbary strain we see today; they were smaller, about 15 hands, and heavier. Cavalry of the day wore fairly light armour – a 'lobster pot' helmet, back and breast plate, weighing about 25lbs. They were usually armed with sabre and a wheel-lock pistol. Although tactics were fairly rudimentary, training had to be thorough. The infantry were divided between pikemen and musketeers. Cromwell was one of some 80 captains paid £1,104 each by Parliament to raise men. Money was always a pressing concern for the Army. Cromwell usually paid for his men's requisitioned horses – unless the owner was a Royalist of course!

An orderly troop?

Discipline among Cromwell's troops was famously rigorous. Swearing and drunkenness were discouraged, and preachers accompanied the soldiers. What probably struck contemporaries more forcefully was Cromwell's radical attitude to the men he recruited. As the quote at the start of this piece indicates, to Cromwell a man's social background was less important to him than his moral and fighting qualities. "A few honest men are better than numbers," he said. This ran contrary to received wisdom about officers being gentlemen. In time, the "levelling" and increasingly radical nature of his forces would come back to haunt Cromwell, but that was all in the future. For now many of those who joined in August, 1642, would have done so because of his local reputation. Perhaps some were commoners who hoped Parliament would give them their land back and halt the drainage speculators. They were to be disappointed – but that too was in the future.

Into battle!

Cromwell joined the Earl of Essex, and played a part at the inconclusive Battle of Edgehill in October, 1642. Cromwell returned to Huntingdon, to recruit and train more troops. He was appointed Governor of the Isle of Ely. By the following spring he had up to 2,000 men in arms, forming his first regiment. These were to become his famous 'Ironsides'. In 1643 he was in action at the siege of Crowland, in Lincolnshire, Grantham, Burghley House near Stamford, and the siege of Lynn in Norfolk. The following year Cromwell's men showed their mettle in the Parliamentary victory at Marston Moor in Yorkshire. The stage was set for the creation of the New Model Army in 1645. Cromwell would go on to become head of state of an English republic following victory in the civil wars and the execution of Charles I in 1649. Surely though, when he first started gathering troops in Huntingdon market place on that August day in 1642, nobody could have seen that coming.

17th century **1643**

The siege of Lynn

Norfolk escaped the worst of the English Civil War. Apart from the time when King's Lynn was besieged.

Parliamentary country here, wasn't it?

In the confused early stages of the civil war, the east and London were among the few places where one side gained control. East Anglia's Parliamentarians were organised as the Eastern Association. They did not have had the total backing of the people. As England drifted towards war in 1642 many just wanted to stay out of it, while others secretly supported the king. East Anglia's Royalists stayed their hand for a year before playing it – and blowing it – on a strike at one of the country's major ports. They didn't bargain for the determination of their enemies, who included a little known farmer turned cavalryman named Oliver Cromwell.

How did Parliament get control?

Historians still argue about how much support Parliament had in Norfolk. In the 1630s Puritans had been persecuted by such as the bishop of Norwich, but in 1642 they seized the initiative. Royalist attempts to raise troops in the area were thwarted. But even the most enthusiastic Parliamentarian was unsure of who people would back if the king's army were to arrive in the east. In 1643 the Earl of Newcastle's Royalist force was advancing south. Parliamentary armies were in retreat, as the king made gains in the west and north. By summer, Newcastle's army was in Lincolnshire.

Time to organise some defences

Energetic and determined, Cromwell was aware of the danger. In March, 1643, he rode into Lynn after reports of Royalist unrest. Mayor Thomas Gurlyn promised to root out 'malevolents'. Cromwell left behind arms and ammunition, then rode south. Shortly afterwards Yarmouth MP Miles Corbett, now in London, ordered the arrest of 13 Royalists. They included Hunstanton landowner Sir Hamon L'Estrange and his sons Nicholas and Roger, Sir Robert de Grey of Merton, Sir Charles Mordaunt, of Little Massingham and a Captain Clench. They were never arrested, and their whereabouts were unknown for the next three months. Sir Hamon was an open Royalist. He must have been encouraged by what was happening nearby. In south Lincolnshire the Royalist minister of Crowland kidnapped his Puritan neighbour in Spalding, defying Parliament's troops at the abbey. In July, Newcastle seized Burghley House, near Stamford. Although Cromwell soon retook it, he then had to ride north to the relief of Gainsborough – only to be forced to retreat. He was becoming frustrated by Parliamentary inaction, writing: "If somewhat be not done in this, you will see Newcastle's army march up into your bowels." Too late. On August 13, Lynn declared for the king.

A Royalist coup?

Aided by Mayor Gurlin, who revealed his true colours, Sir Hamon was named governor. He was well organised; according to opponents he had 40 pieces of artillery, 1,200 muskets, 500 barrels of gunpowder and four troops of horse. As the Royalists dug in and extended Lynn's fortifications, they expected Newcastle's relieving army to arrive. Cromwell made for Norfolk, but Parliament's overall response was sluggish. With the harvest beginning, recruits were hard to come by and those that did arrive were of poor quality and badly armed. Nevertheless, Cromwell seized West Lynn in early September, just across the Ouse, and "kept the town in continual alarms" with "shot and granados". Parliament's navy in The Wash blockaded the port, preventing supplies and equipment from reaching the Royalists; crucially, only one ship reached Lynn during the siege. The town was cut off when the Earl of Manchester took command, and Cromwell moved into Lincolnshire. Manchester secured roads and river bridges.

What did the defenders do?

Foraging parties burnt houses in the village of Gaywood. But civilian support was brittle. On Sunday, September 3, an 18 pound shot crashed into the window of St Margaret's Church during a sermon. Minister Mr Hinson and his congregation were unharmed, but shaken. Sieges were terrifying for civilians; if the town fell by storm they would feel the full fury of the attackers. According to the 'rules' of war, attackers were entitled to put anyone to the sword who failed to surrender. Casualties had been light, despite artillery fire and cavalry sorties. It was estimated only 80 people died throughout. That would change if the town was stormed. As Manchester prepared for an assault using boats and ladders, and cut the supply of water to the town, the Royalists defied his calls to surrender.

Where was the Earl of Newcastle?

The final blow for the Royalists came when the earl retreated. When Manchester offered generous terms – and the threat of imminent storm – on September 16, Sir Hamon surrendered "not as fearing the taking of the town, but to avoid the effusion of blood". Most of Lynn's defenders walked free. They were lucky. To avoid plunder, Lynn paid a massive £2,300 indemnity. Sir Hamon was harried and bankrupted for years to come by vengeful Puritans. Despite an abortive attempt by his son Roger the following year, Norfolk would never rise for the king.

17th century **1648**

The Great Blowe

Norwich erupted into violence in 1648. Royalist rioters were blamed, but discontent beneath the surface of the city may have been more to blame.

Wasn't the civil war over by then?

The 'Great Blowe' had its roots in the first civil war. In the aftermath of the king's surrender in the spring of 1646, religious reformers tightened their grip on Norwich life. The colourful traditions associated with trade guilds, the processions, fair days, songs, stage plays and masques of the mayor's day were suppressed. Christmas, with its pagan connotations, was cancelled. On Christmas Eve, 1645, the mayor ordered clergymen not to hold Christmas services and the shops were told to open as usual. The reformers were not satisfied; 'idolatrous' ornaments were left undestroyed, they thundered, and 'malignant' royalist clergymen still allowed to preach. The Rev John Carter, Puritan vicar of St Peter Mancroft, sternly declared in a sermon aimed pointedly at the city fathers: "The rule of the godly should be more severe."

And what was wrong with that?

The reformers were sincere alright, and wanted to create a better 'godly' society. But many ordinary people chafed under the restrictions; they wanted a bit of traditional fun in their lives. Nationally, the picture was confused. Parliament was divided between conservatives and reformers. The Army seethed with discontent. The king escaped to the Isle of Wight, and royalists sensed a change of mood in their favour. Norwich apprentices and tradesmen clamoured to have their voices heard at last. In 1647 they assembled in Norwich's Castle Yard to petition for the return of Christmas. Mayor John Utting was not unsympathetic. A moderate man, he was under pressure from both sides. Like many fair-minded people in troubled times he succeeded only in outraging extremists from both parties. Soon Puritans on the city council, including Sheriff Thomas Ashwell, wanted him out. Travelling to London early in 1648 they called for him to be removed and arrested. As rumours spread back to Norwich, the seeds of tragedy were sown.

Time for a riot?

Utting had many supporters in Norwich. On Sunday, April 23, a petition circulated calling for him to stay as mayor. As unrest grew, word spread that Westminster officials in the city were going to take him to London. The city gates were locked and by midnight a crowd reckoned at 2,000 strong gathered in the Market Place, shouting for 'God and King Charles'. By many accounts, Utting tried to get them to disperse, but events were out of control. The houses of prominent Puritan aldermen were targeted. Ashwell's home was looted, arms and ammunition carried off. At one address, only when the lady of the house distributed beer to the rioters was violence averted. Cavalry under Colonel Charles Fleetwood were summoned from Dereham.

Who were the rioters?

All sorts of people got caught up. Many were small fry, carried away by the holiday atmosphere, the chance to have a beer and cock a snook at authority. Later, the people hanged included a blacksmith, a dyer, a brazier, a saddler and others described in court as labourers. By 3pm on Monday news had filtered through the cavalry were approaching. The rioters decided to seize arms stored at a building used as the headquarters of the County Committee. The defenders bolted the door and fired from the windows, killing a boy in the crowd. The rioters stormed the building, and took muskets, pistols, swords, pikes and armour. By now the cavalry were in St Stephen's, and a running fight had developed. What happened next is confused. Gunpowder had been spilt in the building and people had lighted torches. Some must have been ignited, for the arsenal exploded. Smoke, dust and debris engulfed the city. Officially, 40 people died in the blast, many more were injured, houses were destroyed and the windows of St Peter Mancroft and St Stephen's Churches blown out. It was known as the 'Great Blowe'.

What was the aftermath?

Nearly 300 people were arrested. For weeks afterwards city magistrates heard conflicting evidence as people sought to exonerate themselves. Close to a hundred prisoners were kept in Norwich castle for several months. They were tried on Christmas Day (some kind of Puritan joke?) Most were fined, but eight ringleaders executed. They included saddler Henry Goward, named by many as a leading spirit in the unrest. The men were executed in the Castle Ditches on January 2, 1649. Mayor Utting fared little better. As a second civil war broke out, the mood was ugly. Utting, along with town clerk John Tooley, was imprisoned and fined.

And back in Norwich?

Many people were left homeless. Part of the city was derelict for decades. Both affected churches were repaired. At St Peter Mancroft, a mason named Martin Morley, initially implicated in the unrest, got this lucrative job. The building where the arsenal exploded was beyond repair. It was not until a minister's widow named Mary Chapman paid to have a hospital for the insane built there in 1713 that the area now named Bethel Street revived.

17th century **1667**

Call the Marines

In 1667 a desperate battle was fought on the Suffolk coast. It marked a first appearance for the marines, a then experimental branch of the British military, who fought off a force four times their size.

Go tell it to the marines!

Landguard Fort guarded the East Anglian coast. Then a vital naval base as well as commercial port, the mile-wide harbour controlled access to towns and ports along the Orwell and Stour rivers. It formed the only deep water harbour between the Thames and Humber. Losing it could open up a backdoor to London for an invading army. Until the reign of Henry VIII, Harwich had to rely on its medieval walls for defence. In 1539, as war with France loomed, Henry made plans for its defence. Landguard Point, south of Felixstowe, controlled access to Harwich's harbour entrance. Four bulwarks were built either side of the harbour entrance, to catch any hostile ship in a crossfire. This formed the basis for the later fort which stood on the site, the defences being renovated during the Armada crisis of 1588. They were subsequently neglected, until tension on the continent in the 1620s caused another re-think. The government of Charles I built a new fort at Landguard; a square earthwork with four bastions and a ditch. It was armed with 62 pieces of artillery and could house a garrison several hundred strong. The bastions jutted out to create four points of a star, to support each other against attackers.

Were they any good?

Neglect and erosion took a toll. In the 1650s the east coast was again on the front line. This time the threat came from a new and surprising enemy; the Dutch. Although at one time allies against Catholic Spain, the two Protestant countries fell out over trade competition. From 1652 to 1673 there were three wars between England and the Netherlands. Charles II, restored to the throne in 1660, was persuaded by hawks in his government to declare war on the Netherlands. But the Dutch were no soft touch, and England was poorly prepared. When plague hit the country in 1665-6 morale sunk; despite high taxation, money for ships and sailors had run out. Most of the fleet stood idle at the Navy's main bases – Harwich, Portsmouth and Chatham. As the summer of 1667 drew on, 13 major Royal warships were at Chatham dockyard. They were sitting ducks when, in early June, Dutch Admiral Michiel de Ruyter led his fleet to the Thames mouth. Troops landed in Kent and broke the defensive chains that guarded London, then sailed along the Medway to burn 13 warships at anchor at Chatham and carry others off as prizes. Leaving destruction in their wake, the Dutch headed north. Their next victim would be Harwich.

Anyone there to stop them?

A Dutch-born military engineer named Sir Bernard de Gomme had earlier been sent by Charles II to shore up Harwich's defences. Shocked at the dilapidated state of Landguard Fort, he got to work. The bastions were enlarged, the earthworks re-dug and brickwork created at the foot of the ramparts around the fort to strengthen it. Command of the garrison was in the hands of Captain Nathaniel Darell. He had 100 gunners and 51 cannon. He also had 400 men from the Duke of York and Albany's Maritime Regiment of Foot – the newly formed Marines. This first official outfit of English 'naval infantry' had been created less than three years earlier. A total of 1,200 men were recruited from the Trained Bands of London – a militia that had seen action during the Civil War. They differed from most infantrymen in that they wore yellow uniforms rather than red, they were all musketeers and had no pikemen, and they were trained to fight at sea. On July 2, 1667, they prepared for their first proper battle.

An even fight?

The Dutch force, 2,000 strong, had landed unopposed at Woodbridge the day before, and attacked Landguard from the landward side. But the new defences held. Captain Darell's 500 defenders rained down artillery and musket fire, and the Netherlanders had to retreat. Both Landguard Fort and the Marines had saved what remained of the fleet, the harbour and port of Harwich, as well as the towns and ports along the Orwell and Stour.

What happened next?

The success at Landguard was poor compensation for the Chatham disaster. England accepted a humiliating peace at the Treaty of Breda later that year, and a period of political instability began. It culminated in 1672 with another inconclusive Anglo-Dutch war, including a full-scale fleet battle off Southwold. After that the countries finally resumed friendly relations. Captain Darell went on to become governor of Sheerness. Darell Day is still celebrated locally, and in 2007 a locomotive was named after him. The Marines had to wait until 1755 to be formally recognised, but went from strength to strength, serving the country to this day. Landguard Fort was rebuilt several times, seeing service during the reign of Queen Victoria and subsequently during the Second World War and Cold War. Today, the site, with its curious amalgamation of buildings from different eras, is open to the public. It is also said to be haunted.

17th century **1672**

The Battle of Sole Bay

In May, 1672 Southwold was shaken by a major sea battle.

England vs France – or England vs Spain?

The opposition was provided by the formidable fleet of the Dutch Republic. The English fleet was allied to our new best friends, the French. More than 30,000 men in the allied fleet took on a large Dutch force in a bloody, but inconclusive, scrap off the Suffolk coast. It was part of a series of naval wars fought by England in the middle of the 17th century.

Why were we fighting the Dutch?

Today the three Anglo-Dutch wars are little remembered. Understandably, as they sit incongruously amid the usual series of wars against 'traditional' foes, France and Spain. The motives for going to war were

Armed and ready: An artillery piece looks out to sea on the coast at Southwold.

somewhat convoluted. The Dutch Republic had emerged from a long ordeal of wars of independence fought against the Spanish Empire. As fellow Protestants they had been aided by Queen Elizabeth I, and commercial, cultural and family links between the two countries were strong, particularly in East Anglia. However, the commercial interests of the two expanding nations conflicted. In a world where overseas trade was closely linked to politics clashes between Dutch and English merchants and seafarers took on grave implications. Things came to a head under Oliver Cromwell's Commonwealth. In the 1650s the two Protestant republics went to war. Fought mainly in narrow seas between southern England and the Netherlands, the action centred on officially sanctioned privateers raiding each other's commerce plus some set piece battles between fleets. Briefly, the conflict of 1652-4 largely went England's way. A second war from 1665-7 was fought under Charles II's restored monarchy. This time the Dutch got the upper hand, their ships sailing up the Medway and burning Chatham dockyard. Within five years a third war began. This time it was caught up in the murky world of international politics. Charles II signed a secret treaty with King Louis XIV of France, the brilliant 'Sun King' who built the Palace of Versailles. Louis wanted to subjugate the Dutch, and saw England as a junior partner. While the vast French army invaded the Netherlands, aided by contingents of English troops, the combined fleets of England and France aimed to blockade the Dutch fleet.

An even struggle?

Holland's strength was her fleet. The country's small land mass encouraged naval expansion. Her admirals were outgunned by the superior English, but adept at both strategy and tactics. England's navy was far from the superb weapon it became in the days of Nelson. The intense training, professionalism and loyalty to the corps – the 'band of brothers' – that would develop later were sadly lacking in the faction-ridden Restoration Navy. Many skippers were soldiers chosen for fighting ability or political connections, rather than naval expertise. For example, Charles's brother James, Duke of York, was Admiral despite his lack of experience (in America, New Amsterdam was seized from the Dutch in 1665 and renamed New York in his honour). His vice-admiral was Edward Montagu, Earl of Sandwich, owner of Hinchingbrooke House, Huntingdon. This former Parliamentary soldier was Samuel Pepys' patron at the Admiralty.

Why Sole Bay?

Sole Bay was the main fleet anchorage. The points of Easton Ness and Dunwich were then a mile or more further out to sea than they are today and formed a bay and safe haven that has now largely been eroded. Southwold is today a genteel, picturesque spot, but in 1672 it was home to a no-doubt hard-drinking, roistering naval contingent. In the early hours of May 28, (by the 'old' calendar) 93 English and French ships were at anchor. A total of 34,496 men and 6,018 cannon were on board. The French, commanded by Comte Jean d'Estrees, made up a third of this number. Unknown to him and the Duke of York, the Dutch were no longer at anchor off the Scheldt, but hard on their heels. Admiral Michiel de Ruyter had launched a pre-emptive strike. He had 75 ships, manned by 20,738 men armed with 4,484 guns.

Battle is joined

Tactics were fairly rudimentary. Both sides launched fireships to destroy the other's ships, as the English had done to the Armada in 1588, but once vessels were side by side it became a matter of gunnery. Those on board had to be brave; there is nowhere to run in a sea battle. The Dutch had the advantage of surprise, and the allies were divided. D'Estrees and his ships steered south, followed by Dutch vessels, and fought out a long-range artillery duel. Some said it was a 'misunderstanding', others claimed it was a deliberate ploy to leave the English to bear the brunt of the fighting. (It later transpired Louis had given secret orders to d'Estrees to avoid battle if possible). In the centre the English and Dutch slogged it out from dawn till dusk. The Duke of York was in the thick of it; he had to move his flag twice, finally to the London, as his flagships Prince Royal and St Michael were crippled by enemy fire. The courageous Sandwich was aboard his flagship the Royal James when, surrounded by enemies, it was hit by a fireship and eventually sank. Transferring to another ship in a small boat, Sandwich was drowned and only ten days later his body identified by the Star of the Garter he was wearing. On the Dutch side 'political officer' Cornelius de Witt sat unflinching on the flagship under fire while men were slaughtered around him. Both sides suffered heavy casualties in ships and men, more than 800 wounded from both sides taken ashore to Southwold.

Who won?

Both sides claimed victory. Tactically, it was a draw. Strategically, the Dutch edged it, although they withdrew. The allies never did blockade their coast, and Anglo-French relations were soured. Any chance of a quick victory disappeared both at sea and on land, where the Dutch flooded their polders to avoid Amsterdam falling. England made peace in 1674 amid growing political instability and internal intrigue. There was little lasting nastiness between England and Holland, except it is believed such derogatory phrases as 'Dutch Courage' and 'Going Dutch' were coined at this time. At all events, it would be a mere 16 years before Dutch Prince William of Orange launched a successful invasion of England during the 'Glorious Revolution' of 1688.

17th century **1675**

The sport of kings

To the best of our knowledge only one reigning English monarch has ever won a competitive horse race. According to legend King Charles II did it in the 1670s – twice – at his favourite venue. Newmarket.

The sport of kings. . .

The English aristocracy, particularly the monarchy, has had a long love affair with the horse. Probably stemming from military chivalric tradition and medieval tournaments, horse racing has a long history on this island. Nowhere was it more popular, nor patronised by the cream of society, than at Newmarket. From the 1660s onwards Charles II and his brother James, Duke of York, made the Suffolk town so popular that at important race meetings, much of the government of the day decamped there from London. In the long run it made the town the centre of world horse racing. The origins of competitive horse racing go back to the 12th century. Knights returning from the crusades in the middle east introduced swift Arabian horses to England. As more Arab stallions were imported, they were bred to English mares – and a new breed of swifter equine sports stars developed. Private wagers among the nobility saw large sums of money changing hands.

Why Newmarket?

Historians have speculated that the surrounding flat heathlands were ideal for racing horses, and indeed that the first to do so may have been Boudicca's Iceni tribe in the 1st century AD. It's tempting to believe the queen's war horses, used for pulling her chariots that so terrified the Romans, were bred and trained nearby. Charles II's grandfather, James I, was the first to use land at Newmarket for racing horses. The first recorded race at the Suffolk town took place in 1622, when Lord Salisbury's horse beat that of the Marquess of Buckingham for a then huge £100 wager. James's son, Charles I, introduced the first cup race at Newmarket in 1634. Royal patronage helped establish the reputation of the sport, but civil war in the 1640s was a setback. Oliver Cromwell's Commonwealth banned racing for money, so equine punters the length and breadth of the land were no doubt delighted when Charles II was restored to the throne in 1660.

Let the good times roll!

There were a number of venues holding races in southern England, but Charles spent most of his time on the course at Newmarket. Near the end of the modern

High Street the Rutland Arms Hotel stands on the site of the king's old palace, and nearby are his stables. After his marriage to Portuguese Catherine of Braganza, he inherited territory in Tangier, north Africa. From there he brought in more Arab stallions, to be bred to produce generations of race horses. He fed them on beer and fresh eggs. Newmarket was suddenly the most fashionable place in provincial England. In 1665 the Plate race was inaugurated there as the king revived the sport and took it on to become a national institution. The diarist Samuel Pepys wrote in May, 1668: "The king and the Duke of York and the court are today at a great horse race at Newmarket". A year later he recorded that the court had all got up at three in the morning to make the trip – a fairly common occurrence such was their enthusiasm. Important national business was often carried on there. In September, 1677, Charles's nephew, William Prince of Orange arrived from Holland

Merry monarch: Charles II had plenty to be happy about whenever he went racing at Newmarket.

on a state visit, and had to prise the king and his brother from the races. The Rowley Mile Racecourse was named after the king, who took the name of his favourite horse, Old Rowley, as an affectionate nickname.

Punter, owner – or jockey?

All three. At one time, on top of a hill on the town heath, was the "king's chair" where he watched horses exercising on Warren Hill, where champions are still put through their paces. Other owners set up shop in East Anglia. The poet and courtier John Evelyn wrote in his diary in 1670: "We were to see the stables and fine horses, of which many were here kept at vast expense with all the art and tenderness imaginable". Away from the course, the races had their social side, and every fashionable young blade about town was there, "racing, dancing, feasting and revelling" in the words of the dour Evelyn. Royal mistresses, such as the famous Nell Gwynne, were also bound to put in an appearance. Nell had a house close to the king's stables. All in all, everyone was having a good time.

What about the locals?

The town boomed. Local tradesmen must have been rubbing their hands, but the less well-off also benefited. Course rules dictated that prize winners should give a sum of 20 shillings "to be distributed to the poor on both sides of Newmarket". Charles was a popular figure there, frequently being observed "mixing himself among the crowd". The king referred to Newmarket as "the sweetest place in the world", revelling in the town's informality where he "allowed himself to put off the king".

And the king's winner?

The story goes that in April, 1675, Charles rode a horse called Blew Capp to victory in the Plate race, repeating a feat he had earlier achieved four years earlier. Sadly, we lack firm evidence that Charles actually rode the winner – but it would be churlish to deny the king his moment of glory.

And today?

Our present Queen enthusiastically keeps up tradition by breeding racehorses in Norfolk, and is a frequent visitor to the town. Newmarket has 2,500 acres of heath and woodland devoted to racing and training horses. Charles II would be at home.

■ In November 2016, Queen Elizabeth II opened the new National Heritage Centre for Horseracing and Sporting Art. Built in the remains of Charles II's sporting palace and racing stables, it is in the centre of Newmarket. It incorporates the National Horse Racing Museum and The Fred Packard Museum and Galleries of Sporting Art.

17th century **1698**

A matter of honour

Just off the B1149 Corpusty to Norwich road stands a stone urn. It marks the scene of the last duel fought in Norfolk.

Rapiers at dawn?

Early on an August morning in 1698 Sir Henry Hobart, of Blickling Hall, 4th baronet, former MP for King's Lynn, and Sir Oliver Le Neve, a lawyer from Great Witchingham, met at Cawston Heath. In a time when a gentleman's honour was a matter of life or death, they fought. Although duels were not always fatal, this one was. Behind the story lies a sub-plot of Norfolk politics – and an unlikely victory for a left-handed underdog.

Who did the fighting?

Hobart owned Blickling. His ancestor, the 1st baronet, having made his fortune through the law, spent it building his magnificent mansion near Aylsham. Despite 3rd baronet 'Old Commonwealth' Hobart's stubborn espousal of republicanism, the family thrived following the restoration of the monarchy in 1660. Young Henry had been knighted by Charles II in 1671 aged just 13. Hobart was a politician; after serving as William of Orange's Gentleman of Horse at the Battle of the Boyne in Ireland, he represented the borough of King's Lynn in Parliament. As a member of the Whig party, he prospered in the political climate of the 1690s. Oliver Le Neve, by contrast, was of more humble station. A Tory-supporting lawyer, he was a country sportsman, fisherman and well-known local drinking man, every inch the Tory 'king and country' squire. Hobart, the court sophisticate, was renowned as a swordsman. He was also argumentative, "dictatorial and headstrong", with a record of disputes with his neighbours. Easy-going Le Neve was better liked, which was to stand him in good stead.

What were they arguing about?

In 1698 a bitter political battle broke out in Norfolk. Hobart had splashed out heavily on an election campaign – spending enough to increase his family's already impressive debts – but had been defeated. He attributed his failure to rumours circulating about his conduct in Ireland during the 1690 Boyne campaign. It seems accusations that Hobart had been a coward were circulating – and Hobart blamed Le Neve. Hobart issued a challenge by letter and in person, but Le Neve denied being the author of the rumours. He wrote to Hobart: "I am ready and

A matter of life and death: The urn marking the spot where two men fought a deadly duel at Cawston Heath in 1698.

desirous to meet you when and where you please to assign . . . for the matter shall not rest as it is though it cost the life of your servant, Oliver Neve".

How did duelling work?

The practice grew out of the medieval legal tradition of trial by combat. As long as the rules were followed, the law usually took a lenient view. Participants were meant to issue formal letters to one another and appoint seconds to make sure fair play ensured. It was considered a disgrace if a man did not answer a challenge, so Le Neve had little option but to fight if he wanted to retain his reputation. Sometimes when opponents met an apology was offered and both parties went away, honour and life intact.

Not this time. Who won?

A betting man would have had his money on Hobart – but he would have lost. As neither man had engaged seconds, the only witness was apparently a servant girl hiding in the bushes. The duel was fought on a Saturday morning; apparently Hobart wounded his opponent in the arm, but his sword got caught up in Le Neve's coat. Le Neve thrust his sword into Hobart's belly. This proved a mortal wound, and the baronet was carried back in agony to Blickling where he died the next day. It is said his dying groans still ring out around the house. (Presumably they don't get mixed up with the other famous ghost. Anne Boleyn is said to also haunt the house, her supposed birthplace).

What happened next?

As no seconds were involved, it was an illegal duel. Le Neve fled to Holland, fearing Hobart's powerful and vengeful family would secure a murder conviction. He stayed there until the heat died down. After living under a series of assumed names he returned, stood trial and was duly acquitted at the Thetford assizes in April, 1700. Perhaps it was thanks to a favourable jury, his good reputation with his neighbours coming to his aid. Hobart left a widow, heiress Elizabeth Maynard, and a five-year-old son. The widow's anger was assuaged when she remarried; her son inherited, the family regained its fortunes and his son later became ambassador to Russia. Le Neve settled back into his country squire life. Apart from fishing, horse-racing and gardening his main occupation was his prized pack of hunting beagles, supposedly the best in England. A Justice of the Peace, he was also a captain in the militia. Tragedy marred his final years. His second wife Jane, who he'd married just a few weeks before the duel, died in 1703 and he remarried a few years later. He chose a London heiress, but she died soon after the marriage. Oliver died of apoplexy in 1711, shortly after the death of his only surviving son, Jack. The duel stone was later put up in the garden of the Woodrow Inn. This is now a petrol station and garage. The Le Neve family home, Great Witchingham Hall, was bought by turkey tycoon Bernard Matthews in the 1950s

How long did duelling go on?

Gradually, society's attitude to violence changed. By the mid-19th century it had gone out of fashion. That didn't stop the Duke of Wellington, when Prime Minister, fighting a duel in 1829 with Lord Winchilsea. Both men deliberately fired wide, and Winchilsea grudgingly apologised. Honour was satisfied. By the Victorian era courts took a less lenient attitude to duels, and the practice died out.

■ **The Cawston Heath duel stone is maintained by the National Trust near the Woodrow garage. Henry Hobart's home at Blickling is open to the public. www.nationaltrust.org.uk**

Walpole to the rescue

Financial crisis and growing panic had gripped the nation. Only one man could save the day – a Norfolk squire named Robert Walpole.

Solid, dependable sort of chap. . .

Financial panics are nothing new. They are the flip side of capitalism – in its infancy during the early years of the 18th century. There was frenzied speculation on the new money markets. In his book The Ascent of Money, historian Niall Ferguson likened the behaviour of people involved in financial ups and downs to that of cattle; herding instinct investment and massive optimism ending in stampedes of panic. Thus it was with the South Sea Bubble. The company was set up to trade in South American ('South Sea') markets, and for a while all went swimmingly. People from high to low backgrounds rushed to put their money into the company's stock. Britain was just ending an expensive war against France and Spain, and the government was keen to pass on its debt to the new company. In return it granted it exclusive future trading rights on the promise of lucrative business with Spanish colonies, including the slave trade – an issue which bothered few at the time. Despite the fact the company was doing little business, the prospect of making money for nothing drew in punters by the thousand.

Not Robert Walpole presumably. . .

He joined in the craze at first, but had the benefit of a canny banker, who advised him to get out while the going was good. Born in 1676 in Houghton, near Fakenham in Norfolk, Robert Walpole was a member of a long-established, influential local Whig family. The Walpoles and the Townshend families dominated mid-Norfolk politics, and it was inevitable that Robert should be elected to the 'family seat' of Castle Rising in 1701. He moved on the following year to King's Lynn, which he represented for the next 40 years. By the end of May, 1720, the South Sea Company's share price had risen from £128 at the start of the year to £550. MPs, government ministers and King George I's mistresses were among those busily investing – at preferential rates – while other punters had to pay the full rate. Insider trading? Absolutely. The whole thing smacked of corruption, and was heading for an almighty crash. Other companies cashed in; one advertised itself as "a company for carrying out an undertaking of great advantage, but nobody to know what it is". In the short term, it proved popular.

By the end of the summer South Sea stocks reached their peak at about £1,000. By that time the clever money, including Walpole's, had already made a sharp exit. There was no trade to make money on; speculation was based on false pretences. It was an empty bubble waiting to burst.

And so to the crash. . .

As markets fell in France and Holland, panic spread to London. South Sea stocks dropped to £150 in late September. People who had taken out huge loans to pay for stocks in the summer now found they could not pay them back. Bankers and aristocrats were drawn in along with ladies' maids and other working people, who wasted their life savings. As thousands faced ruin, Parliament was recalled in December. With so many members of the government implicated – including chief minister Earl Stanhope, along with Chancellor of the Exchequer John Aislabie – storm clouds were gathering, threatening national stability. The Hanoverian king, who spoke no English and had only been on the throne a few years, turned to the only man keeping a cool head. Robert Walpole.

The height of his career

The Norfolk man had undergone political tribulations during the previous decade. At one point his enemies had succeeded in having him imprisoned in the Tower of London. But this country squire, with his deceptively hearty and bluff manner, knew how to play the long game. Appointed First Lord of the Treasury at the height of the financial storm in 1720, he began the task of restoring order. He confiscated the estates of the directors of the South Sea Company and used them to help its victims, while its stock was divided between the Bank of England and the East India Company. Gradually, confidence and stability returned – which was what was needed. The public were in a vengeful mood. At one stage it was proposed tying the guilty parties in a sack filled with snakes and throwing them in the Thames. Walpole's Parliament responded in time-honoured fashion. It held an inquiry and kicked it into the long grass. Some members of the government were found guilty of corruption; some, such as Aislabie, were imprisoned. They were convenient scapegoats lacking powerful allies. Others, such as Walpole's old enemies Stanhope and Sunderland, were protected by his skilful tactics in the House of Commons. For this Walpole gained the epithet 'screenmaster general'. He didn't like them, but it suited him to shield them from punishment as they were close to the Hanoverian monarchy. By protecting the royal family and its friends from scandal, he gained the eternal gratitude of George I. This was vital in his rise to power and keeping hold of it for the next two decades.

What was the legacy of the Bubble?

Walpole was Britain's first 'prime minister' (originally a term of abuse) for 21

Steady as she goes: Norfolk squire and the man who became our first prime minister, Robert Walpole, helped calm fears after the scandal of the South Sea Bubble.
Illustration: Annette Hudson

years. He was a realist and a pragmatist. Famously, he declared that 'every man has his price'. Along with his fellow Norfolk landowner and brother-in-law Townshend, he imposed his own kind of rule over Britain. He dominated Parliament and ensured the country stayed at peace. During his reign he built his magnificent Palladian mansion at Houghton, near Fakenham. He fell from power in 1742 when the one event he could not control – war with Spain – brought about a different kind of madness to that he had cured in 1720-1. Financial crises have been with us ever since. Isaac Newton, himself a loser in the 1720 crash, declared he could "calculate the movements of the stars, but not the madness of men".

A Jacobite tragedy

Tragedy: The plaque in Aylsham telling the story of Christopher Layer.

Christopher Layer's reckless life ended bloodily in 1723. Aged 40, he was hanged, drawn and quartered for high treason. The only memorial to this enigmatic man is an inscription in Aylsham marketplace honouring Norfolk's only militant Jacobite.

What was a Jacobite?

The term comes from the Latin for James, namely James Stuart, King of England until 1688. After he was expelled by William and Mary in the 'Glorious Revolution' Jacobite was the term used to describe those in the British Isles who wanted to see James – or a representative of the House of Stuart – back on the throne. In the 1715 and 1745 risings the Stuarts still had adherents in Britain willing to lay down their lives for the 'king over the water'. The problem was religion; they were Catholics, but England and Scotland were determinedly Protestant. Even then there were many Protestants who believed in the 'Divine Right' of kings.

The Tories?

Many Tories certainly believed this, and would have gladly supported a Stuart monarch if it were not for their Catholicism. Although they disliked the Hanoverian dynasty, which came to rule in 1714, they could not stomach the thought of a Catholic on the throne. Christopher Layer was a Tory, of a Norfolk family from Booton, near Aylsham. His uncle, also Christopher, was Sheriff of Norfolk under Charles II. That all changed in 1688 when he refused to take the vote of allegiance to William of Orange. Those who took this line were known as 'non-jurors' and could not hold office. This did not stop the family making a comfortable living. Young Christopher, born in 1683, attended Norwich Grammar School and was articled to an Aylsham attorney, Henry Rippingall. In 1709 he married Elizabeth Elwin, of Aylsham, and inherited his childless uncle's estate.

So far, so unexceptional

The life of a country attorney wasn't enough for this "vain, hot-tempered and restless" individual. In 1715 London beckoned, and he was accepted to Gray's Inn and the Bar. He lived lavishly, running up debts and getting into bad company. He was forced to sell his Norfolk estate to make ends meet. By the early 1720s Layer was a fully-fledged Jacobite. George I and his Whig ministers were unpopular. James II's son, now known as James III or the Pretender, looked a popular alternative – and Layer thought so. Early in 1721 he and another plotter travelled to Rome and met the Pretender. Layer produced lists of prominent men who would help in a coup d'etat. It was all fantasy; many of the people he mentioned had no intention of supporting such a move. Nevertheless, armed with the blessing of the Pretender, Layer returned to England and began drawing up plans. Having made contact with prominent Jacobite noblemen, he tried to 'turn' Guards officers, including Ensign Erasmus Earle, from Norfolk, who later testified against him at his trial. Having no luck there he enlisted a pair of desperados. Adventurer Steven Lynch was to seize Prime Minister Robert Walpole and the commander of the Army, while Matthew Plunkett was to recruit and arm fighting men. Both took Layer's money, and betrayed him.

Was he naive? Or just a dreamer?

We don't know how serious Layer's plan was. Lynch and Plunkett turned themselves in for the promise of a free pardon, and Layer was arrested in September, 1722. His house was found to be full of weapons. At his trial he bravely refused to turn anyone else in or give any more details, and took many secrets to his death. He never let on about the extent to which the Duke of Norfolk and Lords North and Grey were involved in his schemes. The authorities needed to do little to convict him; Layer had written everything down. He had planned to capture the Tower of London and Royal Mint, arrest the King and Prince of Wales and arm the mob. It took the jury half an hour to find him guilty.

A traitor's death

On May 17, 1723, Layer dressed in his best black suit and was taken to Tyburn. He made a calm speech to the crowd calling for a Stuart restoration before being hanged, drawn and quartered. His head was fixed on a pole above Temple Bar. His sad story later appealed to an Indian prince exiled to Norfolk. In 1908 Prince Frederick Duleep Singh had a plaque at Layer's former Aylsham home, later a branch of Barclays Bank, inscribed:

"Christopher Layer of Booton lived here. He was a faithful adherent of the House of Stuart and for his loyalty to that cause suffered an ignominious death at Tyburn 17th May 1723. Be thou faithul unto death."

Turpin rides into town

In 1737 a seemingly respectable horse-dealer named John Palmer set up shop in Long Sutton, on the Norfolk-Lincolnshire border. This man had a secret. He was none other than the notorious highwayman, Dick Turpin.

Dashing, glamorous sort of chap?

The legendary figure of Dick Turpin fits the bill. A romantic rogue with an air of chivalry, he has cropped up in books, folk ballads and film, entering our national consciousness. But the real Richard Turpin was a killer with a sadistic streak; a poacher, rustler, smuggler and torturer. On the other hand, he was tough and resourceful, and possessed some panache. He certainly knew how to make an exit. By the time he turned up in Long Sutton he was a wanted murderer with a price on his head.

Okay. . . but he probably loved his mum!

Turpin was born in September, 1705. Some accounts say he was born in Finchley, then a village north of London, but he was baptised and grew up at Hempstead, Essex, where his father, John, kept an inn. We know little of the young Turpin, except

Stand and deliver: Dick Turpin turned up – incognito – in Long Sutton in 1737.

that he was apprenticed to a butcher in Whitechapel, married his childhood sweetheart in 1727 and set up in business either as a butcher or an innkeeper. Whether from poverty, an inability to earn an honest living, or sheer devilry, he soon turned to crime. He began with a little bit of poaching – some oxen – then moved on to smuggling, which was then rife throughout the country. For a time it seemed he was living rough, in caves along the East Anglian coast, robbing for a living. But things got really nasty when he joined a group of house-breaking thieves known as the Essex Gang. Their favoured targets were isolated farmhouses. Their favoured persuasive tactic was to torture people into giving up secrets of where they had hidden valuables. In one notorious incident they threatened to burn an aged widow alive; in another they beat a man's wife and daughter until he revealed secrets of where his money was hidden.

A lawless society?

Georgian England had no standing police force. Detection of crime was a haphazard business, depending upon poorly paid constables. On the other hand, in the early years of the 18th century the death penalty was brought in for relatively trivial crimes. Thus, stealing and rustling were capital crimes. Many guilty men went free, but many innocent ones hanged. Life was hard for the poor, and many held anti-establishment views. Attitudes to criminals were ambivalent; some, such as the London thief Jack Sheppard (1702-24) were treated as folk heroes, and some highwaymen attained a spurious glamour. It seems the golden age of the highwayman had already passed; in the years following the end of the Civil War many former Royalist soldiers took to the road. When the Essex Gang broke up, some were caught by the constables. Turpin escaped. With that he joined the ranks of the highwaymen.

A touch of glamour at last?

For a while Turpin and some confederates preyed on stagecoaches in Epping Forest. Then, by chance, he met one 'Captain' Tom King. The 'Captain' was everything Turpin was not; polished, well-mannered, a bit of a toff. Nevertheless, the two went into business, taking to the road around London and East Anglia. They ventured into Norfolk and Suffolk. On one occasion, outside Bungay, the story goes that they came across two young women who had made money selling livestock in the town. King decided they were too pretty to rob; Turpin had no such scruples. He committed his first murder in the spring of 1737, killing a gamekeeper. By now he had a price of £100 on his head. When King was killed in a shoot-out with constables at a London pub, Turpin went on the run.

From London to York?

The legend goes that he rode from the capital to York in 15 hours. Historians now believe this story has been confused with that of an earlier highwayman, John Nevison, who accomplished a similar, though unlikely, feat in 1676. Turpin's route north was an altogether slower one. Which is why, in 1737, he turned up in Long Sutton. People in the market town, west of the River Nene, little suspected that John Palmer was not a horse trader, but the man sought by the authorities. Turpin stayed about nine months in the town, selling horses he had most probably stolen. Legend has it he lived at what is now the Bull Hotel, which dominated the then thriving market place, subsequently at a cottage in the town's High Street. His activities were highly suspicious though, and he was arrested. Not for the first time he escaped, and rode beyond the Humber. This time he ended up in Brough, near Hull. He lived a double life; country gentleman by day, and livestock rustler by night, operating across the county line in Lincolnshire. In the end it was a drunken escapade that did for him. Inebriated, he shot a neighbour's gamecock, and was imprisoned. Inquiries began as to John Palmer's true identity.

It's a fair cop...

From York prison he sent a letter to his brother in Essex, asking him to act as a character witness. But his brother was too mean to pay the sixpence for the letter, and it was opened by the village postmaster. He was the same man who had taught Turpin to write, and recognised his handwriting, complete with false signature. With this information Turpin was found guilty, not of highway robbery, but horse rustling. With the last of his money he shelled out on a new suit and paid for people to act as mourners. On April 7, 1739, he rode in an open cart from prison to what is now York racecourse, bowing ironically to the crowds. On the scaffold he faced the hangman – a former confederate who had turned 'King's Evidence' to save his own life. The York Courant reported: "With undaunted courage he looked about him, and after speaking a few words to the topsman, he threw himself off the ladder and expired in about five minutes".

What next?

Turpin was immortalised in a 19th century novel, then taken up by subsequent generations. The rest is history, though not entirely accurate. In Long Sutton his association is remembered in a street named Dick Turpin Way. The Bull, sadly, is currently boarded up. Turpin may not have been the romantic figure we would like to think he was, but he surely knew how to put on a show.

18th century **1737**

Tom Paine's Thetford

Thetford's best known son was born in 1737, but has had a mixed reputation in his homeland.

A prophet without honour in his own country?

These days Thomas Paine's reputation is riding high. Praised as a democratic hero and a man ahead of his time on both sides of the Atlantic, it is a far cry from 200 years ago when he was condemned as a traitor in Britain. Even in the second half of the last century the suggestion he should be honoured with a statue in Thetford caused uproar.

Why the controversy?

Paine lived in interesting times. Born in Thetford on February 9, 1737, in modest circumstances, he was to alienate many British people with his radical writing and sympathies. He was to support revolutions aimed against his own country – in America and France – which led to indictment for treason in the 1790s. That was all a long way off when he was born in White Hart Street. The Thomas Paine Hotel is the starting point for what the tourist authority terms the 'Thomas Paine Trail', taking in many of the town's historical sites. The house in which he was born is now occupied by the hotel. His father was a corset-maker and smallholder, Joseph Paine, a Quaker. The radical influence of the Society of Friends – leaders in spreading the message of equality, and campaigning to end slavery – must have had an effect on young Thomas. You can see Paine artefacts at the nearby Ancient House Museum of Thetford Life, then see where he went to school. Paine's father was a freeman of the borough of Thetford, which enabled him to send his son to the grammar school at reduced fees. There has been a school on the site since Saxon times, reflecting Thetford's long history.

What kind of childhood did Paine have?

He must have encountered the first inequalities which later galled him while at school, for his family were not rich. He later wrote: "My parents were not able to give me a shilling beyond what they gave me in education and to do this they distressed themselves." On leaving school, aged about 13, he had a better education than most boys of his class. He was apprenticed to his father, but was destined for higher things. The corruption he later lambasted was all around him. The town was dominated by a narrow clique, more interested in its own affairs than benefiting Thetford. As late as 1809, it was disclosed that a member who had not attended a meeting for three years had been absent because he had moved to South America! While local government stagnated, Thetford's Parliamentary seats were controlled by powerful aristocrats – the Duke of Grafton and Lord Ashburton. By the 18th century Thetford had become a byword for a 'rotten borough', where at one time just 31 electors in a population of 1,500 sent two MPs to Westminster.

An angry young man?

Paine tried several jobs – as sailor, schoolteacher and exciseman – but could not settle. Influenced by his friend Benjamin Franklin, the spokesman for American colonists at loggerheads with the British government, his future course was set. In 1774, aged 37, he set sail for America, and was thrust into a propaganda war, leading to revolution. An effective writer, Paine was probably the first to use the term 'United States of America' and his words helped sustain American morale during the War of Independence. Back in England in 1791 he wrote his best-known work The Rights of Man, a defence of the French Revolution and a call for democracy. Paine demanded votes for all, abolition of monarchy, religious toleration and an end to war. With Britain fighting for its existence against Revolutionary France, such sentiments were dangerous; he had to flee for his life. Making for France, he was initially hailed as a hero, but later came close to being guillotined during the Terror. Despite this he wrote The Age of Reason, reiterating his call for religious freedom. He died in America in 1809, controversial to the end.

Why is he important?

Paine is seen as an early democrat, a fearless freethinker who would not be silenced by oppression. His reputation has grown, particularly in the USA, since his death. His quotes have the power to inspire: "These are the times that try men's souls"; "Wealth is no proof of moral character, or poverty of the want of"; "All hereditary government over a people is to them a species of slavery, and representative government is freedom". "Tyranny, like hell, is not easily conquered."

What other sites in Thetford have Paine connections?

The Carnegie Room in Cage Lane is built on the site of a thatched meeting house built by the Society of Friends, where Paine's father worshipped. Just along the road is the town's library, which hosts one of the best collections of Paine material in Britain, available for study by appointment. Which leads us to that famous statue in King Street. The impetus came from America. During the Second World War thousands of US airmen were stationed in East Anglia. An American aircrew from Kenninghall named their B-17 Flying Fortress bomber Thomas Paine.

Radical: The statue of Thomas Paine in Thetford.

Concerned at the lack of recognition for their hero, they also put up a plaque on the Thomas Paine Hotel, then a private residence. Twenty years after the end of the war the American Thomas Paine Society offered to put up a gold statue of their man in his home town. The idea was not universally popular, sparking fierce opposition which received national headlines. The uproar led eventually to the creation of the Thomas Paine Society of Britain – and greater acceptance. The statue was designed by Sir Charles Wheeler in 1964, and stands outside the historic King's House. It depicts Paine holding a pen in one hand and a copy of The Rights of Man in the other. Strangely, the book is upside down, which Wheeler claimed he did to pique onlookers' curiosity.

18th century **1759**

Pilgrim's progress

In the middle of the 18th century a religious phenomenon affected people in England. The spiritual revival ignited by John Wesley sparked extreme reactions nationwide – and in Norfolk.

Who was John Wesley?

He was an Anglican clergyman, born in north Lincolnshire in 1703, himself the son of a clergyman. At the time joining the Church did not necessarily mean you needed a vocation. Partly in reaction to the extremism of the previous century, such "enthusiasm" was frowned upon as dangerous fanaticism. Educated at Oxford, Wesley's life was marked by spiritual seeking. In the 1730s, following a disastrous mission to the new colony in Georgia, America, he found his calling. He formed the first evangelical movement. Although he never left the Church of England he and his followers were at odds with it, and took to preaching in the fields and streets, as most were not ordained. Wesleyans soon aroused strong emotions, for and against. Wesley's message was a radical one. He felt the Church of England was neglecting its duty, allowing people to lapse into lives of wretchedness, and so preached against such abuses as drunkenness. He was attacked by ministers from the pulpit, who accused him and his followers of being Dissenters and fanatics. They disliked his outdoor preaching and use of unordained preachers. Hostility spilled over into mob violence. Nevertheless, Wesley gained converts after people heard him preach.

What was so special about Wesley?

John Nelson, one of his lay preachers, described his charismatic effect as follows: "As soon as he got upon the stand, he stroked back his hair, and turned his face towards where I stood, and I thought fixed his eyes upon me. His countenance struck such an awful dread upon me, before I heard him speak, that it made my heart beat like the pendulum of a clock; and when he did speak I thought his whole discourse was aimed at me." Beginning in Bristol, then spreading to London, Wesley's early allies included his brother Charles and fellow Oxford evangelist George Whitefield. Taking his message further afield, Wesley rode thousands of miles on horseback, often preaching two or three times a day. He took his message to people ignored by the establishment, including prisoners. He was frequently threatened, but his extraordinary charisma helped to deflate the

Charismatic: John Wesley took his message to the people in the 18th century.
Illustration: Annette Hudson

most violent of situations. The same was not always true for his followers, dubbed Methodists for their 'methodical' habits.

A warm welcome?

Incidents from two towns in the early 1750s illustrate the problems faced by Methodist preachers. Samuel Larwood was the first man sent to Norwich, but he only stayed a fortnight. In February, 1752, an unlicenced preacher, James Wheatley, was set on by a mob in the Castle Ditches. Although protected by supporters, the mob was reckoned more than a thousand strong. Wheatley was eventually rescued by the mayor's officers after some rough treatment. Subsequent trouble in Norwich included riots and demolition of a meeting house. In one horrific episode a woman was raped, a pregnant mother kicked to death and a man whipped through the streets wearing a crown of thorns. John and Charles came in July, 1754, and Charles stayed on. The brothers were attacked by members of the Tory

Hell-Fire club, who met at The Bell hotel. At Yarmouth preacher Thomas Olivers was the first Wesleyan in town. Wesley said the port was "as eminent both for wickedness and ignorance as any seaport in England". Sure enough, Olivers had a rough ride. In the narrow Rows, where houses encroached upon one another, women pelted him with basins of water and what was euphemistically described as "dirt". On the open street Olivers was "assailed with such a shower of sticks, stones, turnips, potatoes and apples as he never witnessed before or since". It was only when a sympathetic army officer, Howell Harris, a Welsh Methodist, offered the support of his troops that Olivers was safe to preach in public. He then did so in the Market Place for several nights. Soon he began to make converts.

Word was spreading...

Wesley made an impact wherever he went. At Swaffham his appearance was particularly memorable. Dotted around the town's historic market place are references to his visit. In 1759 he preached at Westgate House from an upstairs window when the congregation from the chapel was too large. The house was owned by a local Methodist family, the Goodricks. By 1771 he had followers in circuits in places such as Bury St Edmunds and King's Lynn. In that year he wrote in his journal: "In the evening I preached at Bury and on Wednesday rode on, through heavy rain, to Lynn. The people received the word with joy though few, as yet, had any root in themselves." He was impressed by Lynn. "The houses in general are better built: Some of them are little palaces. The market place is a spacious and noble square, more beautiful than either that at Yarmouth or Norwich; and the people are quite of another turn, affable and humane. They have the openness and frankness common throughout the county; and they add to it good-nature and courtesy." It wasn't all bad news in Yarmouth. In 1783 the first Wesleyan chapel in town opened at Ferry Boat Row. By 1790, shortly before his death, Wesley visited Yarmouth and found "a society at peace and much united together". At Norwich that same year Wesley preached to an overflowing house. "How wonderfully is the tide turned. I am become an honourable man at Norwich," he wrote.

What was his legacy?

Within a few years of John Wesley's death in 1791, the Methodist Societies became the Methodist Church. Numbers swelled. At his death there were 72,000 in Britain and 60,000 in America – almost 10 per cent of the church-going population. The movement split into groups, such as the Primitive Methodists and United Methodists. A century after his death numbers peaked at six million in the English-speaking world; today there are about 33 million world-wide.

John Wesley A Biography, by Stephen Tomkins

18th century **1795**

Winter weather

"Last night was the severest we have yet had. It froze so sharp within doors, that the milk in the milk-pans in the dairy, was froze." So runs Parson James Woodforde's diary entry from January 20, 1795.

When winter was winter. . .

Recent mild winters have convinced many that the planet is warming up. A scan of the archives from the late 1790s and early part of the 1800s illustrates that winters were more severe 200 years ago. Parson Woodforde was vicar at Weston Longville, Norfolk, from 1776 until his death in 1803, and assiduously recorded weather details. Thanks to people like him, our picture of winter weather at this time is more comprehensive than in earlier days. Harsh conditions were the norm, particularly in the 1790s, notable for cold winters throughout Europe. The following decades saw little improvement. For example, on February 11, 1807, the Norfolk Chronicle reported a heavy fall of snow blocked the roads. On the same day several ships were wrecked during a severe gale on the Norfolk coast. "HMS Snipe came ashore on the South Ham, with 30 French prisoners on board, many of whom, with part of the crew and some women perished." Sixty people died in all. Twelve vessels were wrecked between Cromer and Yarmouth. The following February it was a similar story. "The coaches that should have arrived on Friday did not reach Norwich until the following Tuesday and Wednesday." Fortunately there were heroes at hand. "The mail guards were obliged to traverse the country with the bags on their shoulders, sometimes on foot, up to their breasts in snow. Labourers were employed in clearing the highways, and in some places they cut three miles through the snow."

The mercury was falling. . .

January, 1814: "On the 9th at nine pm the thermometer fell 20 degrees below freezing point, and the severity of the frost rendered the river impassable between Norwich and Yarmouth." More snow blocked the roads between London and Norwich, and the mail coaches were again held up. This cold period continued until late February, when a temperature of minus-17 was recorded on the 25th. There was no let-up in the following decade. In January, 1827, Norfolk temperatures fell 14 degrees below freezing. Not only humans were suffering. "Many hundreds of rabbits perished in the Thetford and Brandon districts through being out in search of food and unable to find their burrows again." Three years later, west Norfolk got it badly. Snow in the Lynn district was "almost up to the lamp-irons". The London mail coach ran into a drift, and was rescued by agricultural horses.

All bets off on a white Christmas!

In 1836 "Christmas Day was ushered in with snowstorms and hailstorms, thunder and lightning." By Boxing Day, the snow had fallen 12ft deep in places. "The Ipswich mail coach, which should have arrived in Norwich on Christmas Day, did not reach the city until 11 o'clock on the night of the 29th. One of the passengers, Captain Petre, undertook to walk to Norwich, a distance of 28 miles; he arrived in the city on the 28th." By mid-January a rapid thaw set in – severe flooding hit Norwich and elsewhere. Six years earlier, the River Yare froze over on Christmas Eve. People must have feared the worst, but a sudden change in temperature saw it thaw within three days. Much the same happened in the December and January of 1840-1. A few years later, ice stopped river traffic between Yarmouth and Norwich, Beccles, Bungay and Aylsham, despite the fact there had been no snow.

Ah, the joys of English weather!

On January 20, 1838, after two weeks of hard frost, the mercury hit a new low of minus 30 degrees. "The river at Lynn was a solid bed of ice. From the eastern side to the opposite shores of West Lynn and North Lynn persons passed and re-passed with the same facility as if it had been land". This weather retained its grip throughout February, before a rapid thaw in early March. In December, 1846, deep snow stranded the coaches from Norwich to Dereham, Swaffham and Lynn. Not even the new railway, introduced during that decade, could beat the freeze. In 1849 snow came in on a north-westerly gale, and trains to London and Yarmouth from Norwich were stranded by deep snow drifts. Horse-drawn coaches were mobilised to rescue passengers. The following March, 12ft of snow delayed the railway, creating a drift in a chalk cutting between Narborough and Swaffham.

Why were the winters so cold?

The first half of the 19th century saw the last hurrah of the Little Ice Age. Following a warm period during the earlier Middle Ages, temperatures dipped, glaciers came south, crops failed, and people suffered. Famines, hypothermia and bread riots were rife in northern Europe. Scandinavians who had colonised parts of Greenland and Newfoundland during the warm spell found their settlements wiped out. Experts can't agree on when it began, with some citing the 1300s, while others say it began in the mid-16th century. For example, the first Thames 'frost fair' was held in 1607; the last in 1814. Historians do agree that after about 1850 things warmed up. Today, critics of global warming maintain – controversially – the climate is still recovering naturally from the Little Ice Age.

Fine city: A view of Norwich over the market to the castle. It seems that 200 years ago the county of Norfolk was home to an assortment of colourful characters.

An eccentric county

The past can seem a serious business. But there were enough characters around to entertain – and exasperate – their contemporaries. A trawl through the Norfolk Chronicle of the early 19th century unearths some examples. Perhaps they had taken Norfolk's unofficial motto – "Do Different" – a bit too literally.

Eccentrics and oddballs. . .

William Durrant, a gardener from Oxburgh, had a strict diet. In 1810 it was reported he "yearly eats 1,095 red herrings, chews 18lb of tobacco and, to give his nose pleasure, takes 365oz of snuff." Charles Archer's job was to get up at 6am each day and wake up the landlord of the Two-Necked Swan, in Norwich's Marketplace. He was paid in beer, and it was estimated he drank 319 gallons in 14 years. Poor Archer had not had an easy life; as a soldier in his early years he had a leg shot off at Gibraltar, only for a hog to "snatch it up in his mouth and run away with it". In an age without any kind of social security or pensions, Archer worked without complaint until his death at the age of 81. Nor was disability a setback for two sporting gents. In March, 1815 at Chapelfield, Norwich, a race was held between Thomas Jenner and William Palmer, two men each with a wooden leg. The wager of £1 was won by the former. Then there was 'Billy Boots'. This Lynn shoeshiner, despite apparently being the illegitimate son of a nobleman, worked for 50 years in the town until his death in 1815.

Age was no barrier

Older eccentrics did not lack energy. In 1812 101-year-old John Brown, a Wymondham carpenter, frequently walked 20 miles a day until shortly before his death. A Mrs Fox, at the age of 100, walked from her home in Plumstead to visit a friend in Norwich. . . and then walked home again. Less adventurous gardener Thomas Chesney lived the whole of his 88 years in the same town; "he was never more than four miles from Swaffham at his death". Longevity and productivity often went together; John Lock, of Larling, aged 110 in 1823, had a reputed 130 children and grandchildren, while Hannah Watt, of Ditchingham, counted five generations of descendants, a total of 121 people. Something in the Norfolk air, perhaps.

The last laugh

Eccentricity often showed itself in death. In 1811 John Thompson, a Norwich lamp lighter, died aged 62. "He was buried at St Martin-at-Palace at night, all his brethren of the ladder and torch attending in the funeral procession with their flambeaux to light him to his long home, in the presence of thousands assembled on the plain." New Houghton man John Mitchell died the same year. "His favourite mule, over 34 years old, at the request of the deceased, went in procession to the grave, and was to have been shot immediately after his return, but through the humane intercession of his granddaughter Miss Young the life of the excellent animal was saved." At the burial of a woman named Bumpstead, at Thurlton, "the husband and an ass walked to church next the corpse. . . as chief mourners." When a Blickling coachman was buried an old friend threw a bottle of rum on to the coffin, upon which it broke. "God bless him," said the man, "I have performed my promise as I am sure he would have done had I gone first."

Death was never far away. . .

Ninety-four-year-old John Minns, a Norwich weaver, died in 1815. "He had anticipated the event 16 years ago, and had then his coffin made, which he had kept in an adjoining room, and used as a cupboard." A King's Lynn man named Benjamin Smith placed his own gravestone in St Margaret's Churchyard 10 years before he died, aged 93. All that had been left blank was a space for his age and date of death. Norwich trunkmaker John Coe not only made his own coffin out of soap chests and tea chests; he also made one for his wife – who survived him. Others showed a mischievous sense of humour. Retired businessman Edmund Manning, of London Street, Norwich, spent years promising some of his relatives he would leave them parts of his large fortune – while spurning others and saying they wouldn't get a penny. On his death in 1838 his will revealed it was a joke; those promised money were cut out, those he had insulted got the cash. Rather more generous spirited, though tragically naive, was eccentric spinster Margaret Creake. Her will stipulated she would leave £50 to each homeless person aged over 68 in London; alas, there was nowhere near enough money to cover the pledge. She also promised to leave a shilling to each relative who turned up to her St Andrews house. In the event more than 1,000 people showed up at her home, "the filthiness of which was beyond description".

Funny thing, humour. . .
Our ancestors found abnormality amusing. Those unfortunate to be born with a disability could find themselves in 'freak' shows – but some made the best of it. Take Miss Biffin. "Born deficient of arms and legs, she was exhibited in a booth at Tombland Fair, Norwich, in 1811. She had previously displayed her powers in miniature painting and needlework at the Angel Inn." Miss Biffin made a return visit to Norwich in 1821. The Angel seemed to be the go-to place for these odd feats. A performer named M du Pain "emersed his hands and feet in boiling lead" in front of packed and astonished audiences. Then there was M Louis, a 7ft 6in tall Frenchman, "exhibited" at The Angel in 1827. Not to be outdone, the Two-Necked Swan boasted the "Lincolnshire gigantic youth", a 13-year-old who weighed 18st, and 19-year-old Elenor Fitzjohn, "Queen of the Dwarfs", just 30 inches high.

Lots of strange men. What about the women?
During the Napoleonic Wars a young Dereham woman, "being strongly attached to a soldier in the 24th Regiment of Foot, resolved to follow him to the wars, and habiting herself in a man's attire enlisted by mistake into the 54th Regiment of Foot recruiting in Norwich. Her sex was discovered and her intentions frustrated". Then there was a North Elmham bride, Miss Copsey. At her marriage to a Mr Frost, "the marriage ceremony suffered a delay of two hours in consequence of the bride not having fully made up her mind, which occasioned a large assembly at the church, before whom at last the knot was tied". Perhaps she'd heard about the man who sold his wife. This was quite common in country areas – as readers of Thomas Hardy's novel The Mayor of Casterbridge will recall. A Downham Market labourer named William Howlett did just that, "and delivered her to the fortunate purchaser in a halter in the Market Place". Thirty years later he died, and the pair could get married themselves. A happy ending – for once.
■ **Information from the Norfolk Annals, Vol 1, 1800-1850.**

19th century **1801**

The sinking of the Invincible

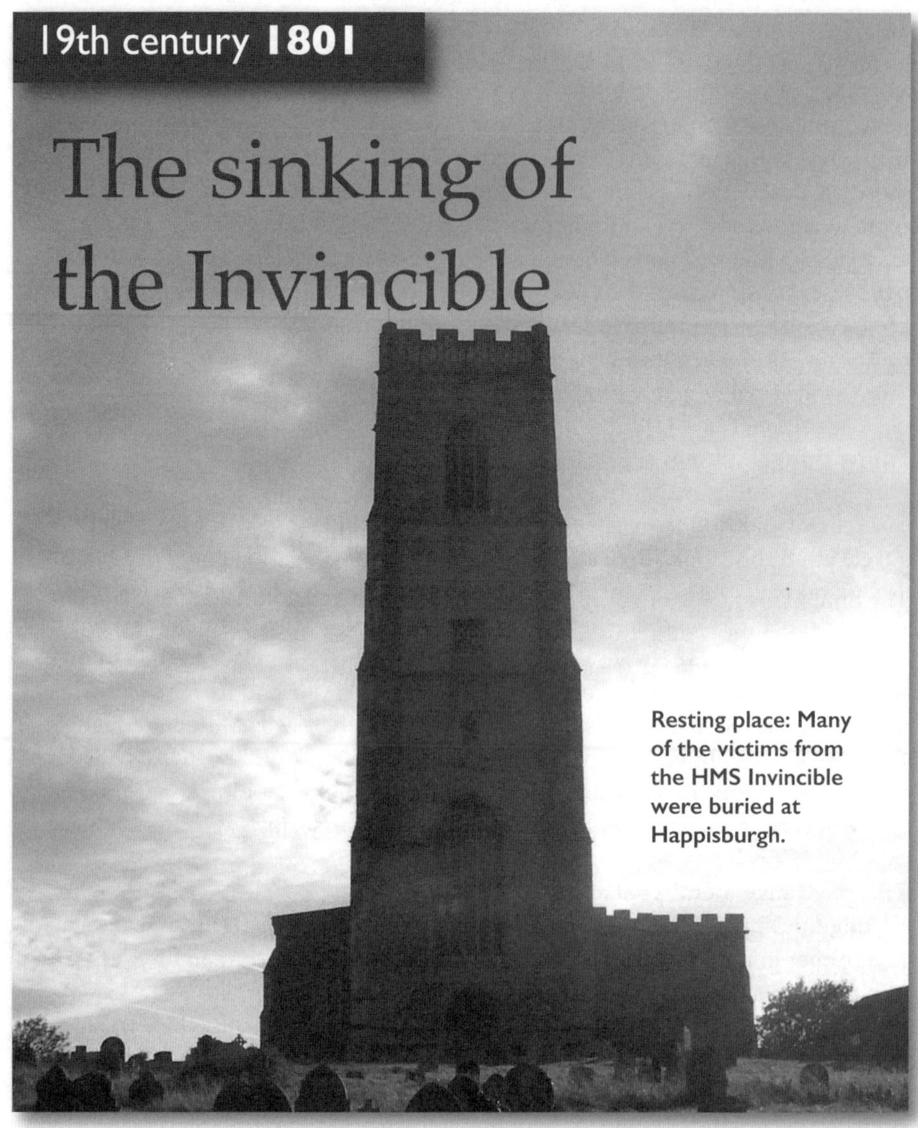

Resting place: Many of the victims from the HMS Invincible were buried at Happisburgh.

HMS Invincible survived nearly four decades of high seas and battles. But she was no match for the treacherous sandbanks off the north-east Norfolk coast. She was not the first – and not the last.

Dangerous waters. . .

Haisbro' Sands, nine miles off the village of Happisburgh, has claimed many ships and lives over the centuries. At one time the sea was so littered with wrecks, divers were sent in to blow them up! Most famous – or infamous – of the vessels lost here was HMS Invincible. She came a cropper in March, 1801, with the loss of 400 of her crew.

Why is it so dangerous?

The north Norfolk coast is characterised by shifting sand bars, lethal to shipping without the knowledge and the right equipment. A bar is long and narrow and develops where the sea deposits granular material, resulting in shallow water. Centuries of shipwreck have acquainted mariners with the knowhow to avoid the places where ships can get stuck, but storms and mishaps will happen. Haisbro' Sands and nearby Hammond's Knoll are particularly notorious. Before 1801 a number of shipwrecks had occurred there. In 1692 a fleet of 200 coal-carrying ships heading from London to Newcastle was blown off the safe Yarmouth Roads onto the sandbanks – 140 vessels were lost. And in 1770, HMS Peggy, a navy sloop, was grounded in a storm, and 32 men died.

Sailor beware!

The officers and crew of HMS Invincible would have known all about the risks. Invincible was a 74-gun third rate ship of the line, with a crew of 590 souls. Third rate does not indicate any kind of inferiority, merely the 18th century Royal Navy's system of designation. A first rate, for example Nelson's flagship HMS Victory, had more than 100 guns and three decks. A third rate had fewer guns, and two decks, but was reckoned an easier ship to handle while still being formidable enough to sink other ships. Launched in 1765, Invincible had seen action at the recent battles of Cape St Vincent (1797), Glorious First of June (1794), and, during the 1780s, at St Kitts in the Caribbean and Chesapeake, off North America. She was a proper veteran. Nor was Rear Admiral Thomas Totty any kind of novice. Aged 55 and born in north Wales, he had joined the Navy at the age of 14, and seen action in the American War of Independence and Napoleonic Wars, in American, Caribbean and European waters. Captain of the Invincible was John Rennie, recently given his first command. Totty was appointed Rear-Admiral on January 1, 1801. He sailed from Yarmouth that March aboard his flagship, the Invincible, bound for the Baltic. He was to join the fleet of Admirals Sir Hyde Parker and Horatio Nelson in an attack on Copenhagen.

Hoping for good weather, no doubt

Guided by local pilots through the Haisbro' passage, strong tides and freshening winds forced Invincible off course. On the afternoon of March 16, she hit Hammond's Knoll. Pinned down for several hours, she finally broke free only to be grounded on a sandbank, where the winds and the waves tore at the mast and started to break the ship up. The crew tried frantically to save her. They cut away masts and manned pumps through the night. It was to no avail. To her aid came a passing fishing vessel called The Nancy. Skippered by Daniel Grigson, she had a catch of cod aboard, but she now loaded up with the youngest members of Invincible's crew as the doomed fight to save the ship went on. Invincible launched her own boats, but the strong wind drove them out to sea. At dawn the next day, Invincible was finally floated into deep water, but sank despite The Nancy's bid to save more of her crew. Some of the lucky ones who had got off on Invincible's boats were later picked up by a coal ship. The rest went down with their ship.

Heavy casualties. . .

Captain Rennie was among those who perished. Admiral Totty was saved, along with 195 of his men. As the next few days unfolded the scale of the disaster became apparent as bodies were washed ashore along the coast. They were gathered up and many of them hastily buried in an unmarked mass grave in ground at St Mary's Churchyard, Happisburgh. As a matter of routine, Totty faced a compulsory court martial. The hearing, at the Royal Navy's base at Sheerness, absolved him and Captain Rennie (posthumously) of all blame. Totty went on to fight alongside Nelson at Copenhagen in his new flagship, HMS Zealous, winning praise from Norfolk's most famous sailor for his efforts. Late that year he was sent to the Caribbean as Commander in Chief of the Leeward Islands Station. Like so many British servicemen in that part of the world, he died of yellow fever the following summer.

And at Happisburgh?

For many years a total of 119 bodies of the crew of Invincible lay in the unmarked grave at the village church. A local resident named Mary Cator tried to get a headstone created, but it came to nothing partly because there were no written records of where the bodies lay. Two decades ago, however, skeletons were found during the digging of a drainage trench. After the captain of the Navy's most recent HMS Invincible, an aircraft carrier, was contacted a stone was given jointly by the ship's company and the parochial church council in 1998. The Invincible's crew now have a fitting memorial. The modern Invincible was the seventh ship of the Royal Navy to bear the name, and served with distinction during the 1982 Falklands War. She was decommissioned in 2005 and eventually sold off for scrap. The seas off Happisburgh continued to present dangers to shipping, with Customs and Revenue cutters sinking there in 1807 and 1822. The list of victims went on throughout the century, with even more ships falling foul during the two world wars. Today, improved equipment and navigation prevents many wrecks, but the City of Sunderland, a cargo ship carrying more than 600 cars, ran aground there in January, 2008. It was eventually refloated with the aid of tugs.

Waiting for Boney

In the early 19th century Britain braced itself for invasion. In East Anglia they were particularly vigilant.

Saved by the English Channel?

Britain was at war with France from 1793 almost continually until victory in 1815. The 1790s had seen the country on alert for French invasion, but this had only happened when an army landed in unsuccessful support of an uprising in Ireland in 1798. Peace in 1802 seemed to signal an end to invasion scares, but the truce was shortlived. Within a year the country was back at war with Napoleon Bonaparte's French empire.The coastal counties of Norfolk and Suffolk expected to find themselves in the frontline. As Napoleon, aka 'Boney', built up an army of occupation on the other side of the Channel, and Nelson and the Royal Navy kept up a vigil to stop them landing here, the home front woke up to the threat and mobilised into action. Across the country even those who had once supported the French Revolution, such as the Whig liberal politician Charles James Fox, took up arms against the imperial designs of "the Corsican ogre".

Were they up to much?

Britain always had a small standing army. By the early 19th century the island state could rely on its powerful navy to deter attack,

Invasion plans: The shadow of Napoleon Bonaparte loomed over East Anglia in the early 1800s.

while hastily improvised militias took care of home defence. Although the British army's continental campaigns had gone badly on land, at sea the navy was unbeatable. But by 1803 it was dawning on people that the threat from Napoleon must be taken seriously – and if the vast French army could somehow evade the British naval blockade there was little to stop them conquering the country. East Anglian counties, with their long coastline, looked very vulnerable. Early that year visitors from the continent who had witnessed "the immense preparations which are now making for the invasion of this country express astonishment at the apathy and indifference which prevail here", according to the Norfolk Annals. But things were changing. In July, 1803 the deputy lieutenants and magistrates of Norfolk, instructed by the government, began planning for the invasion. Marquis Townshend of Raynham was Lord Lieutenant – the Crown's representative in the county. He divided Norfolk into 13 divisions under a lieutenant. Each division was sub-divided into hundreds, under a magistrate, within which each parish came under "some gentleman, clergymen, or principal farmer".

Dad's Army?

Soon troops were a familiar sight across the region. In 1588, with the Spanish Armada in sight, men with pike and musket had drilled on Chapelfield in Norwich. Now, in 1803, their descendants followed suit. In August soldiers of the 47th Regiment of Foot arrived in Norwich to begin training the Army of Reserve – once again in Chapelfield. All were volunteers. Public subscription amounting to more than £6,000 helped fund the troops, and soon in excess of 1,000 men had come forward. At Great Yarmouth a further 500 volunteered. By the end of August 7,300 troops had been raised. A few weeks later, "the Norwich volunteers, commanded by Lt Col Patteson entered the Market Place, and after marching round the Hall and saluting the Corporation, had their colours presented to them by the Mayor." The most non-military of people volunteered, among them Norwich theatre actors, who "agreed to enroll themselves to learn the use of arms". Troops came from all over the county. The Norfolk Volunteer Infantry was divided into battalions from King's Lynn, Wells-next-the-Sea, Cromer, Aylsham, Yarmouth, Norwich, Loddon, Diss and Swaffham. There was even a Norwich Juvenile Regiment, cadets armed with dummy muskets and tin bayonets.

What was the strategy for defence?

Particular care was taken to defend Yarmouth. This vital port and naval base became the centre for a large permanent garrison. Fears were raised it might be attacked in order to deny its use by the Royal Navy. In October the men of the Norwich Volunteers were paraded, and a letter was read out from the Lord Lieutenant asking if they agreed to be permanently garrisoned at Yarmouth. "The officers and gentlemen laid their hands on their breasts, as an appeal to their honour to undertake the duty whenever they should be required". With that they marched off to the coast. Telegraphs, signal flags and tar barrels to be ignited in case of enemy sightings were placed in churches and other high ground along the coast to set up a chain of early warnings, much as had happened in the time of the Armada. Norwich was also garrisoned and its defences improved.

What about supplies?

Merchants offered the use of horses and waggons for the military. In July, 1803 transport company Messrs Marsh and Sons of Norwich and Cambridge offered, in case of invasion, "100 horses, 12 broad-wheeled waggons, 24 men as drivers and assistants, and 24 boats". The ladies of Lynn organised themselves that winter into making flannel underwear for the town's volunteers. Not everyone was so enthusiastic. Early in 1804 a Loddon volunteer named John Baker was drummed out of the corps for refusing to take the oath of allegiance to the king. "His arms and accoutrements, together with the Volunteer clothing, were stripped off on parade, much to the satisfaction of the whole corps".

What about the Royal Navy?

The navy remained vigilant. Late in 1804 a Captain Hancock seized a French privateer (commerce raider) off Yarmouth. Its crew of 98, including its notorious commander Blackman, were marched through Norwich under guard on their way to the prisoner of war camp at Norman Cross, near Peterborough. Volunteers for the navy were hard to come by, as conditions at sea were harsh. In May, 1805 the press gang was unleashed in Yarmouth to gather recruits. "Ships' parties stopped every person they met without discrimination or respect for appearances. No less than 300 persons were impressed". Taken forcibly on board ships in the harbour, eventually all but 50 of the men were released.

What happened next?

The volunteers were never put to the test. In the end the only casualties on land were some soldiers who died by accident during mock battles. Nelson's naval victory at Trafalgar in October, 1805 proved decisive. The news did not reach Norfolk until November 7. Relief was mixed with sorrow, as Nelson died in the moment of victory. "The bells were rung throughout the day, but all the joy. . . was wholly absorbed in sorrow and regret for the death of the Hero". Napoleon broke up his invasion fleet, and marched his army east. He went on to defeat the combined Austrian and Russian armies at Austerlitz, ensuring the war would drag on. The invasion threat to Britain diminished, as the French Emperor's navy went into its shell and Nelson's successors reigned supreme. As with the Armada in 1588 and Hitler's Germany in 1940, the English Channel proved the best means of defence.

19th century **1816**

A year with no summer

The summer of 1816 was a disaster. Heavy rain and storms destroyed crops, harvests failed and subsequent deprivation led to social disorder. It was a phenomenon that affected much of the world. It was the year without a summer.

Early example of climate change?

Experts now broadly agree the weather was down to a massive volcano explosion in Indonesia, that had a knock-on effect across much of the globe. For people living in eastern England in the summer of 1816, the problem was local and immediate – and it threatened their livelihoods and even their existence. The Norfolk Annals record the worst of the weather. On July 18, "after a week's continuous rain, which greatly impeded the hay harvest, a severe thunderstorm occurred. On the 31st the crops were beaten down, acres of turnips were washed away and in several villages the lanes were full of water. On August 12 there was another heavy rain, and on the 31st a hurricane blew, wrecking many colliers between Blakeney and Mundesley. The rains continued to the month of October, when, in consequence of the low lying lands being under water, all hopes were abandoned for the favourable termination of the harvest."

What caused it?

In April, 1815, Mount Tambora erupted. This 13,000ft tall mountain on the island of Sumbawa, Indonesia, blew its top in what was reckoned the greatest volcanic eruption in 1,600 years. By the time it was over, the mountain was 4,000ft smaller and had ejected vast amounts of volcanic dust into the earth's upper atmosphere. The eruption coincided with a period of low solar activity – thus accentuating the effects of blocking out the sun. This came on top of a series of other large volcanic eruptions within a few years, in the Caribbean, Japan and the Philippines as well as Indonesia. The world's climate was disrupted, though it was not until the following year the real effects were seen. China and India's monsoon season went haywire, leading to catastrophic flooding in 1816, while in North America they saw snow the following June. Southern Europe also suffered terrible weather, damaging harvests. In Britain much of the country was affected, especially in the west. Lack of sunshine saw average summertime temperature in England in 1816 fall to 13.3C, the third coldest ever recorded. East Anglia got off quite lightly, but this was the agricultural bread basket of the country, and depended for its prosperity on agriculture. It was in dire straits.

What were the effects?

Social and economic conditions were already harsh. The end of the Napoleonic Wars had seen thousands of soldiers and sailors demobbed – and arrive home to find few jobs and low wages, if they could find any work. Farmworkers bore the brunt of the hardship. For them and their families it became a battle for survival – a true subsistence crisis we have, fortunately, not witnessed since in this country. The last thing anyone wanted in hard times was bad weather. Social unrest was already bubbling over, and failing harvests tipped them over the edge. In May, 1816, farmworkers in Soham, Cambridgeshire, and Downham Market, Norfolk, rioted. The Soham confrontation was the most serious, with a large group of workers clashing with soldiers. Several died and five men were hanged for their part in the unrest, with many more transported to Australia. A further two were executed following the Downham unrest. It wasn't just farmworkers, but the urban poor who went hungry. In the city of Norwich, working people, many of them weavers struggling to make a living in an economic downturn, rioted over the cost of bread – the core part of their diet – and took direct action to seize flour. "A crowd of people gathered in the Market Place, threw fire balls and broke the windows at the Guildhall," recorded the Norfolk Annals. "They then broke into the New Mills. . . and carried some away in sacks." Twice in the next few days the Riot Act was read and the Royal Dragoons were called out of barracks to disperse the crowd.

How long did this go on?

Three years later harvests were still suffering from extreme weather. For example, in July 1820, another severe thunderstorm with hail destroyed hundreds of acres of crops across Norfolk. "Upwards of £600 worth of damage was done to wheat and barley crops of Mr William Ungless, of Whitwell, near Reepham." None of this helped suffering farmworkers, many of whom were being put out of work by the introduction of new farm machinery in the shape of threshing machines. There was increasing unrest in the countryside.

Anything else?

Artists such as J M W Turner depicted the yellow-ish sunsets apparently created by the volcanic dust in a series of paintings. Similar scenes were observed following the eruption of Krakatoa, off Java, in 1883. It was in the gloomy summer of 1816 that Mary Shelley was with her husband Percy and Lord Byron in Switzerland. Influenced by the foreboding weather she wrote her gothic masterpiece, Frankenstein. On the other hand, in the summer of 1816 it was reported you would have seen lovely, sunny weather in Shetland if you were lucky enough to be there. It's an ill wind that blows nobody any good.

Science versus Bottom

In July, 1820, a crowd of 20,000 fight fans from Norfolk and London went to North Walsham. They were there to see a display of open air, bare-knuckle boxing. It was a golden age for the noble art.

Why so popular?

In an age lacking mass spectator sports, before the rise of the ball games that obsess us today, boxing rivalled horse racing for popular appeal. British enthusiasts embraced the ideas of heavyweight champion Jack Broughton. In 1743 he introduced the London Prize Ring rules.

No kicking, biting or gouging?

Bare knuckle boxing was as tough a contest as you could hope for, but Broughton's rules said if a man went down, the fight was over following a 30-second count. The rules also outlawed hitting a downed man or punches below the waist. Otherwise, it was as you were. Boxing was taken up by the upper classes. By the early 19th century the gentlemen of 'the Fancy' – the unlikely brotherhood of the rich, usually aristocratic patron-gamblers and gnarled fighters from the wrong side of the tracks – adored the sport. Lord Byron, the Romantic poet, was a fan – and a bit of a participator, taking lessons in fashionable London gyms. Vast sums of money were won and lost on fights. The sport cut across classes. During the Napoleonic Wars, boxing was regarded as patriotic – a particularly British sport. Some of the big names of boxing found their way to East Anglia. For example, in 1807 celebrated pugilists Tom Cribb and John Gully gave exhibitions in front of appreciative crowds in Norwich. At the King's Head Inn, Norwich, they were watched by 200 people, including MP William Windham. Local fighters made their mark too.

A slug fest?

Bouts were drawn out and bloody. At Wickhampton, in 1816, a fight between Samuel Smith and James Rushmer went 111 rounds. The previous year Pegg "the noted bruiser" and Fox, a horse dealer of Costessey, slugged it out for an hour, "when the former received such a 'pegging' that he was carried off in a state of insensibility." At Limpenhoe, John Green and Rushmer dished out mutual punishment. "In the first seven rounds the latter received seven knockout blows;

but in the eighth he gave the other such a violent blow that he knocked him out and won". Enthusiasts spoke of 'science', a boxer with superior technique and 'bottom', courage and endurance. A few weeks after the Battle of Waterloo, a "long and scientific battle" took place between Chapman and Ellis on a meadow on the Suffolk side of the Waveney, near St Olaves Bridge. The match fluctuated throughout, as did the betting, but by the 54th round Chapman was weakening. "His left eye was closed, and his head became truly terrific, and had from its swollen state a giant-like appearance". Ellis won a purse of £7. Similarly, in August, 1815, John Bell and Matthew Randall, "known for his skill in gymnastic exercise" fought at Cley. "The known bottom of Bell and tried science of Randall drew a considerable concourse of people." Wrestling was also popular. In 1815 at Kirby "a finer display of science was never exhibited" as 24 'professors' entered the ring. "A smart milling took place between Broughton and Ives. Ives proved entirely destitute of science and was badly beaten".

Any famous names?

Norfolk fighters gained a following. Ned Painter, of Norwich, was one. "A boxer of the old English stamp, a stand-up fighter," wrote contemporary journalist and fan Pierce Egan. In 1817 at Bungay Common, Sutton, 'The Black' fought Painter, who was accompanied from Norwich by a large number of supporters. The purse was £100; £80 for the winner, £20 for loser. Painter, "the best man of the day with Norfolk training" won. The writer George Borrow later immortalised his 1820 bout in his book Lavengro. With up to 20,000 people in the crowd near North Walsham, Painter boxed an opponent named Oliver on a specially built platform. According to a report in the Norfolk Annals:

"A staging about 100 yards in length was erected for the accommodation of spectators, for whom, also sixty waggons were formed in a circle round the outer ring; £50 was collected at the gate, and the sums charged for admission to the seats on the staging produced £80. The greatest order prevailed among the 20,000 persons."

Punters had come from London, and lost heavily as Painter won in 12 rounds.

"His colours (yellow) were hoisted upon a waggon, and he was everywhere greeted with loud cheering."

The Norwich man subsequently announced his retirement during a special dinner held at North Walsham. He went on to act as a second to many other boxers. William Cox was another big draw. In 1818 this Norwich blacksmith and city weaver John Camplin fought at a field near Thorpe Asylum. Another of Cox's fights drew 5,000 fans to Kirby Park. He won in 75 rounds against Christopher Barlee, "the Berghapton Groom". Barlee took his revenge on Cox some time later. Despite Cox being the favourite, Barlee downed him in the 80th "by a tremendous blow under the jaw. Cox's head and face presented a frightful spectacle, and not a feature of his countenance could be distinguished." Cox remained popular. At St

Faiths he tackled a London fighter, Teasdale. There had been some dirty dealings. It seemed Teasdale was a 'ringer' – "brought to Norwich and passed off as a countryman named Johnson". After a hard fight, in front of 5,000, "superior science prevailed" and Teasdale won. But punters weren't happy with the deception, and all bets were declared void. Barlee drew an even greater crowd on another occasion – 10,000 by one estimate – on Tasburgh Common.

Who watched the matches?

High society enjoyed the company of fighters. At Testerton Park, the residence of Major Case, Barlee fought a Norwich butcher called Gales. "Barlee, on being declared victor, immediately planted an oak in the ring in the presence of about 5,000 spectators. The two young pugilists were, by order of Major Case, taken under his hospitable roof and put to bed. A large party of the Fancy had the honour of dining with the Major". At the fight between Bell and Randall, in the crowd were spotted "distinguished characters of the neighbourhood. A handsome subscription was made for the conqueror, who was taken from the ground in a gentleman's carriage." Reporters were taken with the number of female fans. At one of Cox's fights, it was noted "among the spectators was a great number of females". "Several well-dressed women were present" at Painter's fights. Hundreds of women watched Christopher Barlee's bouts, "some of very dashing and many more of respectable appearance to be spectatresses of bloody noses and cross buttocks," recalled one correspondent, adding a bit too much detail.

Any critics?

Not everyone approved, particularly of fights held on Sundays. When, in October 1820, four fights were held on Mousehold Heath, participants and spectators were denounced for this "unchristianlike scene". In 1822, a dyer named Grint and a weaver called Purdy fought near Bishop Bridge, Norwich, Purdy died. Grint was found guilty of manslaughter and sentenced to three months' prison. By the later 1820s the authorities were beginning to crack down on illegal fights. In a time of political unrest, large gatherings were suspected, while drunkenness, pickpocketing and disorder made crowds menacing. In 1826 a magistrate prevented a prize fight at Surlingham, while a parish constable at Bramerton "was almost killed attempting to stop a fight". A magistrate also intervened at Mattishall, despite the presence of "many of the principal gentry of the county". By 1840, after a boxer named Cracknell was arrested at the scene of his victory, it was noted: "That these brutal attacks are fast declining in the estimation of the middle classes may be presumed by the paucity in number and the circuitous route taken by many of them to the battlefield". The days of bare knuckle boxing were ending. In 1867 the Marquis of Queensberry codified the sport, putting an end to its rough and tumble days.

Solid: Peckover House in Wisbech, home of a banking dynasty.

A run on the banks

Panic has gripped bank depositors across the country. Banks are going under, and people are losing their money. In a town on the Norfolk-Cambridgeshire border two young brothers, heirs to a proud family tradition, face a fight to keep their business afloat. It is a time for cool heads.

A banking crisis? Cool heads?

Calm down. It's autumn 1825, not autumn 2008 we're talking about. But there are parallels. The banking crisis that gripped Britain in 1825, and the brilliantly improvised response of the Peckover brothers in Wisbech that saved the day for them, could teach our modern day financial geniuses a thing or two.

What about 1825?

"If any bank fails a general run upon the neighbouring banks is apt to take place, which if not checked in the beginning by a pouring into the circulation of a large quantity of gold, leads to very extreme mischief". This is no recently discovered maxim, but the words of banker Henry Thornton – who wrote them in 1802. Britain's banking system looked very different to that of today. By the 1820s a series of small, private banks had sprung up across the country. In Norwich, for example, the Quaker Gurney family had started out in a small way, founded in 1770 in Bank Plain. Marriage with London banking family the Barclays helped forge the giant corporation of that name. The Gurneys' distant relatives by marriage, the Peckovers, had begun business in the fenland town and port of Wisbech during the 1780s. Jonathan Peckover, originally a grocer born in Fakenham in 1755, had built up a hard-earned reputation for sober reliability. He started by storing people's gold in his strong box, issuing them with a paper receipt promising to pay the bearer on production of the note. People trusted him due to his sound character, a trait of the Quakers who were admired for their honesty. In 1794 business was so good he moved with his family to an imposing property on the town's North Brink. Bank House became his new headquarters. The key, of course, was confidence. If every customer of a bank insisted on withdrawing their money in one go there would never be enough to pay them.

Confidence, yes. Not over-confidence.

By 1825 trouble was brewing. Following three years of credit expansion by the Bank of England its reserves were running low. Bank notes in circulation more than doubled in this time. The good times rolled. But there was a price to pay for fiscal irresponsibility. When first a Bristol bank, then six London institutions, closed in the space of four days for lack of funds, the panic spread across the country. Within months a total of 60 country banks had folded for the same reason, and many more were threatened as they could not turn their assets into hard cash in time to satisfy their spooked customers. Depositors, understandably, saw their hard-earned money going down the drain. They demanded to trade their notes for gold – proper, substantial and tangible money for the real economy. There was no Government pledge to protect funds in those days, so people faced ruin. Thornton's law of 1802 came into force. Another rule – if you see a queue of people at your bank removing all their cash, join that queue.

Some cool heads, please

William and Algernon Peckover had been trained well by their father. They were 35 and 32 years old respectively in 1825, and in charge of operations although old Jonathan still had eight years left to live. No time for novices? These two siblings had banking in their blood. That December they rose to the occasion. Algernon took the family carriage and rode as quickly as possible to London. There he swiftly called in every favour the family had built up over half a century of trading, and returned with a large hoard of gold coins. Travelling overnight up to Wisbech, the brothers opened their doors in the morning. As expected there was a large crowd of anxious investors. The bank's shutters opened slowly, adding to the tension. They were greeted with a display of agricultural sacks overloaded with coins. Above them was a banner reading "your money back", "and a Peck-over". Reassured, the customers went on their way. This bank, at least, weathered the storm.

What happened elsewhere?

Under Government pressure, the Bank of England acted as lender of last resort. It pumped an unprecedented amount of gold into the economy, lending as never before, and the panic eased as confidence was restored. A number of reforms were brought in designed to prevent such outbreaks of banks over-extending themselves. The Peckovers continued to thrive in Wisbech. On their father's death William and Algernon became partners. They were intimately involved in the town's affairs, endowing parks and hospitals in the area. Algernon's son Alexander became Lord Lieutenant of Cambridgeshire under Queen Victoria and Baron Peckover of Wisbech.

Any other wobbles?

As events of the past few years have shown, those who forget the mistakes of history are doomed to repeat them. The Gurneys had continued to expand. But by 1866 the firm of Overend, Gurney and Company got into trouble. The company, run by cousins of the Norwich family, was floated during a stock market boom in the early 1860s. But by early 1866 the boom was over. In May, the bank was bust, along with others. A contemporary journal noted: "A terror and anxiety took possession of men's minds". Once again, the Bank of England had to pump money in to ease the panic. The Times reported that Gurney's Bank of Norwich were in the clear. "That establishment recently passed into the hands of new partners, whose resources are beyond all question". The Peckovers narrowly avoided being dragged in. Despite building up their gold stocks, two days of brisk withdrawals drained them. With crisis looming, a well-known and distinguished local customer came in and ostentatiously deposited £100. Panic over. Family partnership in the bank ended in 1893, and it became a branch of Barclays when Gurneys merged, along with other Quaker banks, three years later. The family remained locally important, and the last of the Peckovers died in 1948.

■ **Peckover House stands on the North Brink in Wisbech, and is a National Trust property open to the public. You can also enjoy the gardens there which the family treasured. Octavia Hill's Birthplace House is on the opposite side of the river. She was one of the founders of the National Trust in 1895.**

19th century **1827**

The Resurrection Men

In December, 1827 more than 20 bodies were stolen from a churchyard in Yarmouth. The Resurrection men had come calling.

Bringing the dead to life?

'Resurrection men' was the term commonly applied to body snatchers. By the early years of the 19th century they were feared and hated the length and breadth of the country. Although the most notorious case occurred in Edinburgh, in Norfolk popular frenzy was unleashed against their actions.

Why snatch bodies?

A law passed in 1752 allowed doctors and medical practitioners to cut up certain corpses for educational purposes. Only murderers could be sentenced to death and dissection. In the 18th century a dearth of medical schools and a plethora of executions meant supply met demand. By the early 19th century an average of 55 people were hanged each year, but the growing number of medical schools needed at least 500 corpses for dissection. The Resurrection men met this demand, supplying fresh corpses to doctors, many of whom had to balance their ethical distaste with their need to learn more about anatomy. The crime of body snatching was a misdemeanour, which meant it merited only a fine and/or imprisonment, rather than a felony, which carried the death penalty. But, if they stole jewellery or clothes from corpses, it could become a felony, and they might hang for that. As it was a lucrative business, there were plenty willing to take the risk of detection, particularly as the authorities might turn a blind eye to what some saw as a necessary evil. Charles Dickens, in a Tale of Two Cities, depicted the part-time Resurrection man Jerry Cruncher as a bit of a lovable rogue.

Not everyone agreed. . .

Understandably, relatives of the dead were outraged by this sacrilege. In the late 1820s a backlash began against body-snatching. It was exacerbated by the case of Burke and Hare in Edinburgh. They had taken to murdering people in order to provide really fresh bodies to a Dr Robert Knox. Their arrest and conviction sparked an outcry. The Norfolk Chronicle reported, on December 29, 1827: "Great excitement was caused in Yarmouth by the discovery that upwards of 20 recently interred bodies had been removed from the churchyard by Resurrection men. The churchyard was quickly crowded by the population. Wives were searching for the remains of their deceased husbands, husbands for those of their wives, and parents for their children." It was hard to catch body-snatchers, but on this occasion three men, Thomas Smith alias Vaughan, William Barber, and Robert Barber were apprehended. The case was eventually tried the following August at Norwich Assizes before Lord Chief Baron Alexander. Only Vaughan (or Smith) stood in the dock. "Robert Barker turned King's Evidence, and described the method by which the graves were robbed, and how the bodies were sent to London by the wain. A verdict of guilty was returned, and on November 14, 1828, the prisoner was brought for sentence in the Court of King's Bench. He urged that he was driven by poverty to the commission of the offence, and was sentenced by Mr Justice Bayley to six months' imprisonment at Norwich."

Not exactly harsh!

Relatives of the dead weren't inclined to be so lenient. Many took to watching the graves of the freshly buried. On a January night in 1828 a party of grave watchers shot a body-snatcher in Bacton churchyard. "He was in the act of disinterring the body of James Howlett, who was accidentally killed a few days previously. The resurrectionist, although badly wounded, effected his escape in the darkness." Security extended to the grave. At King's Lynn the following February, "an individual who was consigned to the grave had round his coffin 13 iron hoops, and in the lid 50 screws." As well as iron coffins, graves were protected by iron bars. The Resurrection men seemed to be everywhere. One day they struck at Thorpe, the next at Hethersett, then at Hardingham. In September, 1828, the body of Anne Coe, who died two days previously, was stolen from Fincham churchyard. "The churchyard is very near the turnpike road," reported the Chronicle, hinting that the thieves had made off with the body along that road. "The coffin, containing the shroud, was found in the churchyard, superficially covered in mud." That November, a hamper conveyed by Messrs Marsh and Swan's London van from King's Lynn, was found to contain the dead body of a young woman, supposed to have been taken from a grave at Lynn. In 1832, Sarah Watling, buried at Swanton Abbot, was stolen. At the Norfolk Quarter sessions the following March held in Norwich, George Ives and Nathaniel Canham were accused, but acquitted, of the theft. Another macabre case occurred at Lakenham, where 24-year-old Elizabeth Watts was buried in November, 1830. A few weeks later her brother, who had expressed a desire to be buried alongside his sister, also died. When they opened up the grave, Elizabeth's body was missing.

This couldn't go on

Doctors had been pressing for a change in the law. In January, 1829, Norfolk medics had met at Norwich's Guildhall to add their names to the growing clamour for the Government to act. Partly to appease public outcry, in 1832 an Anatomy Act was passed. This made it legal to dissect unclaimed bodies and those donated by relatives to be used to study anatomy by licensed doctors. Among the first to volunteer his own body was the utilitarian philosopher Jeremy Bentham, who died in 1832. The trade ended virtually overnight. There was the occasional, almost farcical, reoccurrence. In 1838 Norwich veterinary surgeon George Perowne was accused of stealing the body of John Maxey, who had worked for him. Maxey's wife Mary claimed Perowne had stolen the corpse from her house and taken it to his surgery. There he cut out the heart and conducted other experiments. Perowne even drove off Mrs Maxey and family mourners when they came to collect the body for burial. "Mr Perowne was too drunk to appear at court, but he was apprehended and taken before the magistrates where he claimed he had paid for the body of the deceased during his lifetime and contended it was his property." He said he acted in the interests of science, although he was not licensed to dissect corpses. Although the case went to trial, remarkably Perowne was discharged.

And today?

Medical research continues to be a prickly subject. Today the practice is overseen by the Human Tissue Authority.

Captain Swing

"Prepare your wicked soul for death".
So read a letter sent to an East Anglian clergyman in the autumn of 1830. It came signed, as many such threatening messages did, by Captain Swing.

A military man?
We don't know who Captain Swing was – or even if he existed. More likely he was a name invented by desperate agricultural workers to frighten those they believed were oppressing them and their families. They had good reason for desperation. In 1830 times were hard for landless farmworkers. In addition to their back-breaking work, they endured unsympathetic employers, who often treated them like cattle, and a harsh penal system which treated working people with great severity. Already, in 1816, in Soham, Cambridgeshire, unrest among farmworkers had reached boiling point, with violent repercussions. The decade and a half following that localised disturbance saw things get even worse for the rural poor.

Why?
Events conspired against them. In the previous half century reforming landowners with an eye to increasing productivity and profit had continued the process of enclosure that denied villagers their 'common land' – areas used communally for crops and pasture for generations. Traditional poor relief had been undermined since the 1790s, a time when war had brought hard times to both town and country. Victory in 1815 against Napoleonic France brought no peace dividends. Thousands of demobilised soldiers and sailors entered a depressed jobs market. Many were working, if at all, for little money. In the growing urban areas workers responded. The mythical figure of 'Ned Ludd' led weavers and spinners into breaking factory machinery. Rural workers, less able to organise, were slow to respond in kind. But when new machinery arrived to make their lot even worse, things finally exploded.

What machinery?
Horse-powered threshing machines could do the work of many men. As more landowners bought them, they threatened the already tenuous livelihoods of workers across southern England. As early as 1804 at Hethersett a machine designed by a Devonshire engineer named Ball was demonstrated, and their use spread quickly. They threw men out of work, and were hated. Following failed

harvests in 1828 and 1829, the winter of 1830 looked ominous. One who saw the approaching peril was William Cobbett. This radical journalist and campaigner saw at first hand the declining living standards across the countryside and spoke out in fury. His Rural Rides of the 1820s exposed the ill treatment of the dispossessed poor, and warned of trouble ahead. Meanwhile, the Church of England still insisted on payment of its time-honoured tithe, the right to a percentage of the harvest. This was now a cash payment which went to the local parson, who was often resented for it. Landowners who had once lived in close proximity to their workforce were becoming socially estranged from them, hiring them only when needed and paying poor wages. The authorities reacted harshly to anything they saw as sedition. Ever since the start of the French Revolution in the 1790s they had feared popular unrest turning into an attempt to destroy the government. Trouble was brewing.

Enter Captain Swing. . .

In Kent threatening messages began to arrive at the homes of farmers who had brought in the threshing machines. This was followed up by rioters breaking them. Unrest spread through the Home Counties, into the midlands and East Anglia. Magistrates, parsons, wealthy farmers and Poor Law guardians were the targets of threatening letters signed by Swing. The Captain demanded wage rises, a cut in the tithe and destruction of the threshing machines. The slogan 'Bread and Blood' was used, and crowds of between 200 and 400 people gathered to make good their threats. Property was the target, rather than people. Machines were wrecked and hay ricks burnt. Historian E P Thompson, in his influential 1963 book The Making of the English Working Class, described the rioters as "curiously indecisive and unbloodthirsty mobs". No-one was killed during the disturbances, despite their widespread nature.

What happened in Norfolk?

According to the Norfolk Annals, trouble started on November 10. The machine breaking and stack firing would gradually spread across the county. The first fire was at the farm of Mr J Hill at Briston. Six days later a mob destroyed machinery belonging to Paston landowner John Girling. "The outrages became so numerous that the principal agriculturalists got rid of their threshing machines," reported the Annals. Other villages affected included Walcott and Taverham, where a paper mill was destroyed. Lord Lieutenant Col Wodehouse ordered special constables sworn in across the county. At Melton Constable Sir Jacob Astley offered a £1,000 reward for the apprehension of offenders. This seemed to make him a target. A few days later local gentlemen came to his aid, intercepting rioters at Hindolvestone making for his land. They arrested the ringleaders, locking them in the Walsingham Bridewell. Trouble flared again, and a message was sent to the

Norfolk Hunt, who were meeting at Elmham Park. The horsemen rode to Melton Constable and dispersed more rioters. The 1st Royal Dragoons were also sent from Norwich to help. Unrest spread to the industrial parts of the city, where sawmills at North Catton and factory looms in St Martin's were targeted. Some people in authority were not lacking in sympathy, while stressing that they would uphold the law. The magistrates in Tunstead and Happing declared:

"Such disturbances principally arise from the use of Threshing Machines, and to the insufficient Wages of the Labourers. The Magistrates therefore beg to recommend to the Owners and Occupiers of Land in these Hundreds to discontinue the use of Threshing machines, and to increase the Wages of Labour to Ten Shillings a week for able bodied men, and that when task work is preferred, that it should be put out at such a rate as to enable an industrious man to earn Two Shillings per day."

Sensible compromise?

Lord Melbourne's Whig government reacted severely. Accusing local magistrates of undue leniency they sent in troops and set up special courts to deal with prisoners quickly. Across England a total of 19 people were executed, and some 1,000 were either transported to Australia or jailed. Gardener Robert West was transported to New South Wales for his part in wrecking the Taverham mill, and died there seven years later. On January 5, 1831, Norwich magistrates tried 108 people. A total of 67 were found guilty of machine-breaking, and imprisoned or transported; 41 were acquitted or otherwise discharged. One was sentenced to 14 years' transportation; eight to seven years. Fifty were charged with rioting and other offences, of whom 23 were convicted. In March Richard Nockolds was condemned at the Norfolk Lent Assizes held at Norwich for stack burning at Swanton Abbott. He was hanged at Castle Hill on April 9. His body was "subsequently exhibited at his cottage at Pockthorpe and a considerable sum of money was in this way raised for the widow".

Did the riots achieve anything?

In 1832 it seemed revolution was imminent. Agitation for Parliamentary reform was spreading throughout the country. The ruling class heeded the warning, and widened the voting franchise in the first great reform act, giving the middle class the vote. Urban and rural workers switched support to the Chartists, who channelled protest towards constitutional reform during the 1840s. But, for farmworkers in East Anglia, life remained tough and they stayed at loggerheads with their employers. Not until Joseph Arch formed an agricultural trade union in 1872 did they have any organisation – and even that proved an abortive exercise.

And Captain Swing?

He remains an enigma, a symbol of a troubled period in history.

The last post

Early in 1846 the last mail coach ran between Norwich and London. It was the end of an era.

On January 17, 1846, The Norfolk Chronicle reported: "All the coaches between Norwich and London have ceased to run". It was the final nail in the coffin of what had been a thriving business for more than half a century. In 1785 the first Post Office mail coach travelled the 116 miles between London and Norwich. It was the start of the golden age of the stagecoach.

An important service

Regular mail deliveries were vital for a growing economy. Although an official postal service had been in operation since 1635, its deliveries were haphazard and inefficient. They were at the mercy of terrible roads, impassable in bad weather, and highwaymen – the scourge of travellers. But an experiment initiated by the government of William Pitt the Younger changed everything. The first mail coaches started operations between the capital and Bristol in 1784. Within 12 months the service had spread to 10 towns and cities the length and breadth of the country, Norwich among them. At first the coaches were contracted to private operators, but soon the Post Office had their own, superior vehicles. Decked out in black and red corporate colours, they became the symbol of the age. Faster and less crowded than private stage coaches, the mail coach could accommodate four passengers inside – paying a premium rate – and others seated next to the driver.

A cushy job?

Sitting at the back of the coach, exposed like the driver to the elements, was the guard. He was an important figure. The only Post Office employee aboard, he was responsible for the safety of the mail. Resplendent in his scarlet uniform, he was armed with a blunderbuss, a brace of pistols and a cutlass. Guards were well paid, a sensible measure to ensure they were not tempted to turn to robbery or collusion with highwaymen. However, an Act of Parliament in 1811 made it illegal for them to fire their gun except in defence of the mail – an act punishable by a £5 fine, which implies some of the guards were a little trigger happy. Comfort for the passengers came second to the safe and timely delivery of mail. At some stops the mail was simply thrown over the side, then the coach rode on. Elsewhere it made stops at coaching inns which sprang up to accommodate the coaches. Inns such as The Maids Head in Norwich did a roaring trade. Apart from providing food and accommodation for passengers they stabled horses and hired out new mounts.

The mail must get through. . .

On the poor roads of the mid-1780s, mail coaches averaged about 7-8mph in summer, 5mph in winter. By the Victorian era, with new turnpike roads making things better, they were up to about 10mph on average. Weather conditions could still block the roads. In December, 1808, a week of heavy snowfall prevented the arrival of the mail in Norwich from London – causing consternation to local business. "The mail guards were obliged to traverse the country with the bags on their shoulders, sometimes on foot, up to their breasts in snow, across the open fields and heaths." The mail coach was often first with the news. In April, 1814, it arrived in Norwich "with colours flying and passengers decorated with the white cockade" bringing news of the abdication of Napoleon Bonaparte and arrival of an Allied army in Paris.

What about the rest of Norfolk?

In October, 1768 a man named Sylas Neville recorded details of a trip from London to Great Yarmouth. He took one of the new 'flying machines'. Starting from central London at 7am his coach reached Newmarket where it made an overnight stop. At 5am it was off north to Norwich, where it completed its part of the journey. Neville stayed at the Maids Head overnight, and took a stagecoach the final 20 miles to Yarmouth the next day. A two-day journey was normal at a time when it was quicker to travel by water than road. As the Industrial Revolution spread nationwide, road building techniques improved. The marshy land between Yarmouth and Norwich was drained, and the new Acle Straight opened in 1831, cutting miles off a journey that had hitherto involved going north from Yarmouth via Caister and crossing the River Bure at Acle to get to Norwich. By the early 19th century the coach took 16 hours to get from Yarmouth to London, via Ipswich; the mail coach from Norwich to Charing Cross left Norfolk at 5pm and got to the capital at 7am – a journey of 14 hours. Other coaches linked other places in Norfolk to the capital. A rash of coaches started up, often in competition with one another. In 1801 the Lord Nelson was advertised, travelling between London and King's Lynn in 14 hours, via Cambridge and Ely. Another coach travelled from Fakenham four times a week, stopping off for supper in Cambridge and riding through the night, arriving at London early the next morning. Meanwhile, the official Lynn mail coach departed daily from the town's Duke's Head inn, stopping at Brandon, Barton Mills, Newmarket, Bournbridge and Epping en route to London.

Don't forget the drivers!

Drivers were a breed apart. It was a feat of skill and endurance to handle the four horses pulling the coach. Many became admired, almost legendary characters. In 1825 The Norfolk Chronicle reported the retirement of a coachman named Thorogood. In his three years at the reins of "The Times" coach he had driven every day from the Norfolk Hotel, Norwich, to the Swan with Two Necks, Lad Lane, London, "a distance of 116 miles without any accident or consequence, a task which was never before performed by any man". It was calculated he rode 182,352 miles, and always slept at The Bell, Orford Hill, when in Norwich. Some drivers had hidden depths. Tom Cross, the 'gentleman whip', driver of the Lynn-London coach, in 1844 delivered a lecture on the plays of William Shakespeare at the town's Assembly Rooms.

But these good times couldn't last forever. . .

The coming of the railways in the 1840s quickly made mail coaches redundant. The end came quickly. The final London-Norwich coach ran in 1846, just two years after Norwich Thorpe railway station opened. The final regional mail coaches ran until the 1850s. "About 700 horses have been thrown off the road," reported the Norfolk Chronicle in 1846.

"During the droving season last year 9,300 beasts were housed at the Bird-in-Hand public house, Tasburgh, and the landlord purchased for their consumption and for horses etc 50 tons of hay; but so great is the diminuation of the traffic occasioned by the Norfolk Railway, that during the present season only twelve beasts have been taken in, and the landlord has had occasion for only eight and a half hundredweight of hay."

It wasn't all over for working horses though. Many were re-employed drawing "omnibuses, cabs and flys" taking passengers to the new railway stations.

Sinking feeling: The Holme Fen Post. When originally driven in to the ground back in 1852 its topmost point was at the level of the ground. It has shrunk 13ft in a century and a half.

Whittlesey Mere

Once it was southern England's largest inland lake. Today, that water has long been drained for agriculture – but it may be about to make a comeback.

Where is it?

Whittlesey Mere is on the western edge of the fens, south-east of Peterborough, near the villages of Yaxley, Farcet, Holme and Stilton. It's hard to believe now that these neat rows of fields, with long straight roads and equally straight drainage ditches – 'dykes' – was once a vast lake. It stretched about three miles east to west and two and a half miles north to south in summer, while winter flooding could make it even larger. Until the 19th century it was a paradise for boaters and fishermen, teeming with wildlife all year around and used by skaters in winter when frozen.

Man-made or natural?

Unlike the Norfolk Broads, now believed to be man-made diggings which later flooded, geologists say Whittlesey Mere was created by nature. About 6,000 years ago forest covered what is now the fens, this large area in parts of Norfolk, Cambridgeshire and Lincolnshire, and prehistoric man hunted in woodlands of oak, yew and pine. Rising sea levels held back river flows, waterlogging the fen basin, and drowning trees. Reeds and sedges thrived in wet conditions and peat formed from the remains of dead vegetation. In low-lying areas it led to the creation of lakes or meres. The skeleton of a killer whale has been found on the bed of the mere. By Victorian times it was seven metres (about 21ft) deep in places. This situation existed for centuries, and a hardy breed of people – the legendary Fen Tigers – lived by water fowling in the soggy landscape. Monasteries were built on islands, attracted by the isolation of the place. After the mere was drained silver treasures from nearby Ramsey Abbey were discovered at the bottom. Although the Romans undertook some small-scale drainage, which was continued in medieval times, it was not until the 17th century that people looked seriously at changing the landscape with large-scale projects.

Why would they want to?

Profit. The fertile peat soil would in time be turned into the bread basket of England, a huge agricultural area to feed a growing population. We are getting ahead of ourselves here. While Dutchman Cornelius Vermuyden, backed by wealthy cash 'adventurers', was busy straightening rivers and draining vast expanses of fenland elsewhere, Whittlesey Mere remained largely untouched. In summer it was a playground for the rich. George Walpole, third earl of Orford, grandson of Britain's first prime minister, sailed a flotilla of nine boats to the mere in 1774 for a month of nautical high jinks, along with the Earl of Sandwich. Humbler folk made the best of the hard winters of the period; from the 17th to the 19th centuries the mere was regularly frozen over. Skating championships were held with big cash prizes offered. It is said a top skater could cover a mile in just three minutes over the ice. Legend says some expert skaters even chased pike seen beneath the ice, racing the fish until they were exhausted, then breaking the ice and netting them. Wildlife such as the bittern thrived, along with geese, swans and herons who hid in the reedbeds. The swallowtail was common there, along with copper butterflies and many other species of fauna and flora.

And then came the adventurers. . .

By the 1840s a group of businessmen – called 'adventurers' as they 'adventured' their money – had plans for the mere. To these hard-headed capitalists, the mere was wasted. It was high time this land was put to work. The usual methods of drainage – digging ditches – proved inadequate, but modern science came to their aid. A centrifugal pump demonstrated at the Crystal Palace in 1851 could get rid of 70 tons of water in a minute. Holme landowner William Wells bought one, powered by a steam engine, and installed it in a pumping station. Soon the mere was dry. Fishermen, boaters, skaters and, of course, the wildlife were left high and dry. A pike said to weigh 52lb – the biggest found in Britain – was among the casualties.

And the results?

A way of life came to an end. The adventurers reaped the rewards. What was once only useful as fen for cutting reeds was now prime agricultural land. Rents soared. But there was another, unforseen, consequence. The peat shrank dramatically once it dried out and was exposed to bacteria and winds. Realising this, William Wells sank an iron post deep into the ground near Holme in 1852. Within 10 years the top of the post stuck out six feet above the ground. This shrinkage continued until the end of the century. It has slowed since, but now the peat has shrunk 13ft in the century and a half since installation. A second post was sunk in 1957. This is the lowest point in the country, seven feet below sea level.

What's in the future?

Birch wood grew as the fen dried up. Some fragments of the original fen are managed by Natural England, which helps rare plants survive. The Holme Fen Reserve posts are surrounded by woodland; it is eerily quiet despite being close to the busy A1 highway and the main railway line. Geese and swans still enjoy a haven in small lakes, ghosts of what used to exist here. Commercial peat cutting in the reserve has led to creation of areas of open water that support birds, dragonflies and marsh plants such as golden dock. More ambitious is the Great Fen Project, a scheme to see 7,000 acres of farmland in the area returned to natural fen. Supported by some local authorities and conservationists, with the backing of well-known people such as the Prince of Wales and Stephen Fry, the plan is to gradually buy back farmland, pump water back in and create a wildlife reserve that could even harbour the likes of the bittern and copper butterfly. By the spring of 2017 more than half of land in the Great Fen was owned by Great Fen partners. An innovative new Visitor Centre is planned to be built at New Decoy Farm, north of the B660 road. The Whittlesey Mere that existed before 1851 might then make a partial comeback.

20th century **1912**

The flooded city

Flooding caused chaos in East Anglia during the summer of 1912.

Stormy weather. . .

August, 1912, was dull, wet and cold throughout Britain. The worst came in the last week of the month. Early on Monday, August 26, a deep depression swung eastwards, settling in just off Cromer. It brought 30 hours of heavy rainfall and gale-force winds, and left disaster in its wake. The north-east of Norfolk was badly hit, especially the built-up areas in and around the north and east of Norwich. At Brundall, 205.5mm of rain fell in a day and a half; four months' of average rainfall in a little over 24 hours. As meteorologist Philip Eden wrote recently, it was the equivalent of 150,000m gallons falling: "As if the entire contents of Lake Windermere had been emptied twice over." The average rainfall across Norfolk was 125mm before the torrent stopped on the morning of the 27th.

Get the sandbags ready. . .

It all happened with terrifying speed. In Norwich streets flooded as the drains were clogged with debris. On August 27 the rivers Yare and Wensum began to overflow. North of the river and off Dereham Road, in places the water stood 4m (12ft) high. Soon water was coming into houses. A total of 4km2 of housing – some 3,650 houses containing 15,000 people – were affected. Meteorologist Arthur Preston was living in Eaton at the time. He described the rainfall as "not a straight, hard thunder-rain, but reminded me more of a blizzard of fine snow. It was in the Heigham and Coslany districts that the cruel floods wrought the greatest misery," recorded Preston. "Many of the streets and roads in low-lying parts of the city are like rivers, and in the cathedral close there is a large lake". In many streets, such as Carrow Road and Magdalen Street, the only means of transport was by boat.

What was the extent of the damage?

Vast areas of the county were under water. Things were at their worst where the Yare and Wensum met. Norwich was cut off by rail and road for two days. The city's gas and electricity supplies failed and trams were suspended. A total of 40 bridges were washed away, including those over the River Chet at Loddon and over the Bure at Horstead. In the Waveney Valley torrential rain and hurricane winds tore at towns such as Beccles and Bungay. The Waveney burst its banks, creating an inland sea, and rail lines were cut to both towns as Gillingham marsh flooded. Thousands of acres of crops were ruined, just as the harvest should have been underway. Cattle drowned, their bloated carcasses eventually being displayed when the water subsided.

The greatest drama was in Norwich

Given the scale of the disaster it is almost miraculous only three people died. City people rallied round. Boatman William Marrison and a policeman named Horner spent 12 hours ferrying more than 100 people to safety as their houses were threatened by the rising water, driven by fierce currents. The pair would have saved more but their boat capsized and they had to save themselves. Both men survived. Fish porter George Brodie saved many near his home in Oak Street, including children. But he was drowned as his strength failed him. A Mrs Kemp, also of Oak Street, died "of fright" as she was being ferried to safety. Baby Edward Pell perished as the boat in which he and his family were using to escape capsized in Ely Street. It took three days to find his body when the waters subsided.

What was the official response?

Schools and other buildings were turned into makeshift shelters for the 2,000 people left homeless. Chocolate makers Caley's of Norwich provided milk and hot chocolate to people trapped in upper storeys of buildings, the supplies lifted up to them by men using poles from boats. As Norwich and its immediate hinterland recovered by August 30, concern spread to Yarmouth and Lowestoft. It was feared the waters of the Wensum, Yare and Bure combined might flood both towns. But the peaty land of the Broads acted as a giant sponge, absorbing the worst of the waters. The vast amounts of debris carried by the water helped to silt up many waterways of the Broads. This damaged their delicate eco-systems and had a detrimental effect on the growing tourist industry. As the clear-up began a relief fund raised £20,000 for the homeless – an immense amount at the time. King George V and Queen Mary contributed, as Norfolk's plight made headlines nationwide. Many houses were damaged beyond repair by damp, and the poor quality of much of the stock was shown up as many had to be demolished. According to press reports one house in three was below the standard laid down by the Local Government Board and one in five not fit for human habitation.

Anything else?

There is a sad postscript. For many years working people in Norwich had kept canaries as a hobby. By the 20th century Norwich was synonymous with canaries – hence the nickname of the football club. Many birds were kept in cages in gardens, backyards and sheds. When the floods came there was little time to rescue the birds, and people were preoccupied with more pressing matters. Thousands drowned. It is believed one strain of Norwich canary was wiped out.

20th century **1939**

The Sutton Hoo find

In 1939, on the eve of the Second World War, Britain's greatest archaeological find emerged in Suffolk. Historians have argued ever since about what exactly was found at Sutton Hoo.

Big ship with a warrior king's burial site, wasn't it?

Seventy years after excavations at Sutton Hoo, near Woodbridge, a fuller picture is emerging. It is an enigmatic find, casting light on a little known era. The tortuous tale of the modern archaeology is just as fascinating as the history behind it.

What's at Sutton Hoo?

It's an East Anglian Anglo-Saxon royal burial site, dating back at least to the seventh century. In 1938 nobody really knew what was there. But wealthy widow, amateur archaeologist and landowner Edith May Pretty was intrigued by mysterious mounds on an escarpment overlooking the Deben river. She hired Basil Brown, a Suffolk farmer and sometime archaeologist, to excavate the site. They were not the first. During the time of Henry VIII and Elizabeth I treasure hunters had cast their beady eyes on the mounds. Yet, despite some 17th century accounts of a golden crown being found, there was nothing substantial discovered. Further digging in the 19th century yielded nothing new, so the odd series of mounds – 17 in all – remained a brooding presence. That changed when 50-year-old Brown and his team of diggers, including Mrs Pretty's gardener, got to work.

Who was Basil Brown?

Brown had been scouring the north Suffolk countryside for years looking for Roman remains. He was employed on a near full-time basis by Ipswich Museum. In the summer of 1938 he was paid by Mrs Pretty to excavate three of the mounds. What he found was the disturbed – probably robbed – remains of a cemetery. The following spring, he made the astounding discovery of a 27-metre (90ft) long ship impression in the largest mound. The wood had long since rotted away, but a 'ghost' outline remained. Excited by the news, a team from the Office of Works arrived in Suffolk. Led by a Cambridge scholar, Charles Phillips, they were from a different background to Basil Brown. Of Suffolk yeoman farmer stock, he was largely self-educated. There was some conflict between the locals who had unearthed the find and the Cambridge men, but, by all accounts, Brown displayed

Saxon king: Who was the important individual buried at Sutton Hoo in Suffolk? Here is the entrance to the National Trust visitor site.

a great deal of common sense and diplomacy that won him wide respect.

What was found?

By August, 1939, it was clear Sutton Hoo was important, and police guarded the site from curious eyes. Within the impression of the ship, with rows of rivets still in place, there had been a wooden chamber containing a full-face helmet, a sword with gold and garnet fittings, a whetstone and stand which may have been part of royal regalia, spears, a battle axe, a shield bearing animal motifs, silver drinking horns, bronze and silver jewellery and utensils and coins from the continent. These coins dated the contents to the years 620-640AD.

Who owned the treasure?

In September, 1939, as Britain went to war with Germany, an inquest decided the grave goods belonged to Mrs Pretty. Unselfishly, she donated it all to the British

Museum. Prime Minister Winston Churchill later offered her an OBE in recognition, but she refused. She died in 1942. Wartime concerns delayed further work. During the war the treasure was stored in the London Underground for safety, while the Army took over the site, which had been filled in. Basil Brown's career was interrupted by the war, but he went back to work for the museum afterwards. He died in 1977.

What happened after the war?

The original consensus that this was a form of mausoleum to a dead chief held for a while, as there was no evidence of a body. However, subsequent investigation, using increasingly sophisticated techniques, told a different tale. It is possible the skeleton could have been erased, and the acid sand at Sutton Hoo may have been responsible. During the 1960s, a six-year excavation by the British Museum revealed more secrets as it became apparent the area had later been used as an execution ground. Subsequent research from the 1980s revealed an increasingly complex tale as more burial sites were studied.

Who was buried there?

Most modern scholars feel it most likely the ship held the body of Raedwald, king of East Anglia, and briefly 'Bretwalda' (High King) of all the English. Although this cannot be proven conclusively, it's just too good a story not to believe. The site is four miles from Rendlesham, power base of the East Anglian kings during their era of independence. The pagan nature of the burial has raised further questions. Raedwald ruled just as Christian missionaries were converting the English. Although he too converted to the new faith, he seems to have been hedging his bets by being buried in this spectacularly pagan fashion. He was part of the Wuffing dynasty – the 'sons of the wolf' – who originally came from Sweden, and this may explain the Scandinavian-style ship burial. It was certainly unusual, a fitting farewell for such an exalted figure. As one modern historian wrote: "Even in those days the ceremony would perhaps have been considered magnificently old-fashioned." In the long run the East Anglian kingdom was too small to survive. Overshadowed by the powerful Mercians from the neighbouring midlands, the last independent king of the eastern Angles was Edmund. He was defeated and killed by the Vikings in 869AD. East Anglia became part of a united England in the 10th century.

What can we see today?

The National Trust's visitor centre opened in 2002 close to the main mound cemetery. You can see a full-size reconstruction of the burial chamber and grave goods. This atmospheric place, described by the Trust as "page one of English history", is set in a 245-acre site with estuary views and circular walks.

The Desert Rats get ready for D-Day

'May the fathers long tell the children about the tale.'
Winston Churchill

By the side of a road running through Thetford Forest stands a replica Second World War tank. It's hard to believe this quiet spot was once temporary home to 14,000 men preparing for the greatest battle in British history.

An out of the way kind of place

Early in 1944 the Seventh Armoured Division arrived in England for the only time in its career. The division had made a name for itself since its formation in 1938 to protect the Suez Canal in Egypt and oilfields then held by Britain. After fighting successfully against Rommel's German Afrika Korps and Italian allies, the division entered folklore as the Desert Rats, named after the jerboa, a small desert rodent. The division took part in the invasions of Sicily and Italy, and was then posted to England in February, 1944, to prepare for the invasion of France – and take possession of the British army's latest tank, the Cromwell. In this remote spot, surrounded by woodland and now hosting a caravan site, a woodland walk has been laid out highlighting the few surviving buildings and remains. A series of informative picture boards with quotes from some of the soldiers involved help give the story a human face. Part of the division – 1st and 5th Royal Tank Regiments and the 4th County of London Yeomanry – were stationed at High Ash Camp. A subaltern, Lt John Lawson, takes up the story of arriving in "deep, anonymous countryside" with only "fir trees, mud and some drab Nissen huts". Trooper Trevor Grundy confirmed this view, referring to the scene as "a wild place". Soon though the NAAFI (Navy, Army, Air Force Institute) moved in to provide rudimentary food and entertainment. The men were housed in Nissen huts, the standard army accommodation of the time; prefabricated buildings of corrugated steel in a half cylinder shape. They were about 27ft (about nine metres) wide, accommodating 18 men at a time. Lack of insulation made condensation a problem, and moving in during February cannot have been fun.

What were they doing?

The purpose of sending the division back to England, apart from preparing for the Normandy landings, was to familiarise the troops with their new tank. The first Cromwells rolled off the Birmingham production lines early in 1944 and were delivered to Norfolk straight away. Their Rolls Royce Meteor engines were modified Spitfire Merlin engines. Many crewmen felt the tank's excellent acceleration and speed proved lifesavers in the campaigns in France and beyond that followed. For now, the men concentrated on mastering the mechanics, wireless and handling of the tank and taking part in a series of mock battles. King George VI reviewed troops at Brandon station as training reached its culmination.

What was life like?

An army marches on its stomach – and the Desert Rats certainly did battle on a full English breakfast. The men arose each day at 6am and breakfasted at 7 on porridge, bacon or sausage and fried egg, baked beans, toast, jam and tea. First parade was in the tank park at 8am, and they went off duty at 5pm – though preparations for the following day could go on till midnight. The camp had to be kept secret from enemy spies and aircraft. This meant a night-time blackout. Lt Lawson recalled: "We learnt to navigate our way to and fro in the dark by the stars, for with so many twists and turns among the trees it was easy to become disorientated."

No time for luxury?

The senior officers had it better. Didlington Hall, two miles to the north, was requistioned as headquarters. In overall command was Major General G W R 'Bobby' Erskine. There was a senior and junior officers' mess at the hall, since demolished. No doubt the men needed to blow off some steam. At weekends crowded trucks took them off to such hot spots as Brandon, Thetford, Swaffham, King's Lynn, Norwich, Newmarket or Cambridge for a night out – but they had to be back by midnight. Sgt John Harland recalled the pubs and cinemas of Lynn "overcrowded with troops", while Lt Lawson escaped the discipline of HQ with the occasional dinner at local pubs, "cheerful occasions and without formality". As the time came for departure to the front, the officers were invited for a regimental dance by Lady Bedingfeld at Oxburgh Hall, near Downham Market. In retrospect it was a poignant occasion ". . . like the dinner before the Battle of Waterloo. Never again were we to meet in this way; too many crossed the Normandy beaches and never saw home again," recalled Lawson.

On to D-Day

On June 5, 1944, the division quit the forest and sailed from Felixstowe for Normandy. The Desert Rats went ashore with their Cromwells on Gold Beach.

Memorial: A replica of Little Audrey, one of the Desert Rats' Cromwell tanks, stands at the entrance to the memorial on the A1065 road between Swaffham and Mundford.

They were heavily involved in the tough fighting from then on, particularly in Normandy, until the following spring, when they reached Berlin. There they were addressed by Prime Minister Winston Churchill, whose words are also quoted on Page 153: "May your glory ever shine, may your laurels never fade, may the memory of this glorious pilgrimage of war you have made . . . never die. It is a march unsurpassed through all the story of war."

And the present day?

Les Dinning, a tank trooper during the war, organised the setting up of a lasting memorial at High Ash. A replica of a Cromwell Mark IV, named Little Audrey, was erected on a plinth by the A1065 north of Mundford. An inscription reads: "From El Alamein to Berlin via North Africa, Italy, Thetford Forest, France, Belgium and the Netherlands". The memorial was inaugurated in 1998 by Field Marshall Lord Carver, who commanded the 1st Regiment on D-Day. An open day is held each June by the Seventh Armoured Division Thetford Forest Memorial Association.

The memorial is on the A1065 road between Swaffham and Mundford.

Select bibliography

Like all writers I owe a huge debt to a variety of primary and secondary sources. Below is a list of some of them.

Sir Gawain and the Green Knight – anon
The Roman Shore Forts – Andrew Pearson
The Anglo-Saxon Chronicles – anon
Ecclesiastical History of the English People – Bede
Beowulf – anon
Folk Heroes of Britain – Charles Kightly
In Search of the Dark Ages – Michael Wood
Collected Ghost Stories – M R James
Medieval Norwich – ed Carole Rawcliffe and Richard Wilson
King John – Marc Morris
Edward I, A Great and Terrible King – Marc Morris
England, Arise – Juliet Barker
Blood and Roses – Helen Castor
Cromwell, Our Chief of Men – Antonia Fraser
God's Englishman – Christopher Hill
Religion and the Decline of Magic – Keith Thomas
The Stripping of the Altars – Eamon Duffy
The Book of Books – Melvyn Bragg
1666 Plague War and Hellfire – Rebecca Rideal
Britain and the World (1649-1815) – J R Jones
A History of Britain – Simon Schama
The Ascent of Money – Niall Ferguson
Norfolk Portraits, Norfolk Gallery and Norfolk in the Civil War – R W Ketton-Cremer
The Rights of Man and Age of Reason – Thomas Paine
John Wesley, A Biography – Stephen Tomkins
Diary of a Country Parson – James Woodforde
Norfolk Annals 1801-1850 – Charles Mackie
The Buildings of England – Nikolaus Pevsner and Bill Wilson
The Making of the English Working Class – E P Thompson
Great British Weather Disasters – Philip Eden